THE AUTHOR: Janine Beichman teaches Japanese literature and theater at the University of Library and Information Science in Tsukuba Science City, Japan. Born and educated in the United States, she received her doctorate in East Asian Studies from Columbia University in 1974 and has lived in Japan since 1969. In addition to her research on Masaoka Shiki, she has published on other Japanese poets, classical and modern, as well as on Nō, which she has been studying as literature and performance for twenty years. Her original Nō play *Drifting Fires* had its premiere performance at the Tsukuba International Science Exposition in 1985 and has been translated into Japanese by the poet Ōoka Makoto.

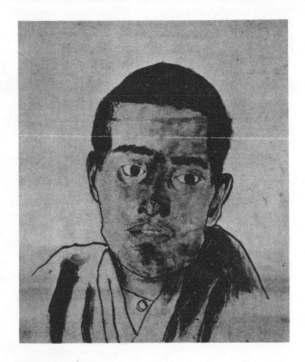

MASAOKA SHIKI
(1867-1902)

Masaoka Shiki

Janine Beichman

KODANSHA INTERNATIONAL
Tokyo, New York, and San Francisco

Previously published by Twayne Publishers in 1982.

Distributed in the United States by Kodansha International-al/USA Ltd., through Harper & Row, Publishers, Inc., 10 East 53rd Street, New York, New York 10022. Published by Kodansha International Ltd., 12-21, Otowa 2-chome, Bunkyo-ku, Tokyo 112 and Kodansha International/USA Ltd., with offices at 10 East 53rd Street, New York, New York 10022 and The Hearst Building, 5 Third Street, Suite No. 400, San Francisco, California 94103. Copyright in Japan 1986 by Kodansha International Ltd. All rights reserved. Printed in Japan.

LCC 85-45310
ISBN 0-87011-753-X
ISBN 4-7700-1253-5 (in Japan)

First paperback edition, 1986

for Aya
and
for Abbie

Contents

Preface

Japanese critics like to refer to Masaoka Shiki as "the father of the modern haiku." By this they mean two things: first, that Shiki was the earliest to write haiku that were modern in both theme and subject; and second, that all the major currents of contemporary haiku have their beginnings in him. Both views are true, but too much emphasis on them tends to obscure other facets of Shiki that may be of even more interest to non-Japanese readers.

The popular image of Shiki is as a haiku poet, but in fact his allegiance from the beginning of his career was never to the haiku alone but to literature as a whole, that new cultural category spawned by the Meiji period. He wrote much tanka criticism and poetry and gave birth to a new school of tanka poetry. In the last few years of his life, Shiki also wrote a series of diaries and essays which became central in the development of the language and diction of modern Japanese prose.

Shiki was one of the first modern Japanese authors to write seriously in several different genres with no sense of contradiction. Many of his contemporaries also did so: Tsubouchi Shōyō wrote plays, novels, and literary criticism; Shiki's friend Yosano Tekkan wrote tanka, free verse, and poetic criticism, and also translated poetry; both Kunikida Doppo and Shimazaki Tōson began as poets but moved on to fiction; Natsume Sōseki and Mori Ōgai, also friends of Shiki, both wrote extensively in several different genres of prose and verse. Shiki, while part of this trend, was also one of its creators, one of the first *littérateurs* (*bungakusha*) of modern Japan.

Born just one year before the Meiji Restoration, Shiki was in many ways a transitional figure, his writings standing midway between the premodern and the modern periods, his character and life partaking of both. Had he lived longer, perhaps the paradoxes of his thought would have been resolved as the tensions engendered by the interaction of foreign and indigenous cultures worked themselves out. Or perhaps they would not have, for Shiki seems to have enjoyed paradox, ambiguity, and irony. At any rate, he was quite unperturbed even when aware of the logical inconsistencies in which they sometimes involved him. His decision to devote his life to the haiku and the tanka, although he believed that both forms would be extinct by the end of the Meiji period, is a case in point. He was aware of the contradiction between his actions and his belief, but in a letter to his friend and disciple Kawahigashi Hekigotō in 1892, he remarked that as an artist he ignored such theories and thought that Hekigotō should, too. In the same way, he sought a justification for Japan's traditional poetic forms (the haiku and the tanka) in Western ideas (Herbert Spencer's), but did not feel free to pursue literature as a vocation until he could make it conform to the rationalism and scholarly approach of the Confucian tradition. In other words, he felt a need to justify traditional poetry in modern terms, and a modern vocation in traditional terms.

In his poetry, too, one often finds a delicate balance of such opposing elements as realism and fantasy, objective description and subjective expression. The theme of several of his most moving writings in prose and verse was the coexistence of two other sorts of opposites—himself dying and the living natural world around him. In his diaries as well he tended to perceive the world itself as a series of dualities, reminiscent of the parallelisms of the Sino-Japanese prose he had studied as a child.

The ability to balance conflicting elements, to hold two opposites in the mind at once—what I would call "dual-consciousness"—was characteristic of Shiki. He himself, at least as a haiku poet, may be seen as a moment in time when such conflicting currents existed in harmony, in a precarious balance of tension, much like a brief peace between warring powers, or the undifferentiated chaos at the beginning of the world (a metaphor suggested by the image of Shiki as a poetic progenitor). After Shiki's death, his two chief haiku disciples, Kawahigashi Hekigotō and Takahama Kyoshi, split into two separate groups. From Hekigotō and his followers came the free-meter haiku, which did away with syllabic rules and gave rise to some of the most innovative modern poets, such as Nakazuka Ippekirō. From Kyoshi came the more conservative current, which conceived of the haiku as

realistic descriptions of nature and from which emerged such poets as
Mizuhara Shūōshi and Nakamura Kusadao.[1]

In the tanka, the development of Shiki's ideas proceeded in more of
a straight line. His stress on observation and his ideas on the sketch
from life were later elaborated into a coherent aesthetic theory by
Saitō Mokichi and others, while in his short tanka and haiku sequences
we can see the beginnings of the longer modern tanka and haiku
sequences.

Most of Shiki's writing was autobiographical. In general, literature
in Japan tends to be more overtly autobiographical than in Europe and
North America. Jean-Jacques Rousseau's *Confessions* would probably
have been considered an autobiographical novel (*watakushi shōsetsu*)
had it been written in Japanese. It may seem an example of the
biographical fallacy to assume that the "I" of Shiki's writings was
identical with Shiki himself, but I have done so because Shiki himself
wrote as if he meant us to take them that way, and also because it is
virtually impossible to distinguish between the real Shiki and the
fictive Shiki. In fact, in the last few years of his life, the fictive Shiki
seems to me to have been necessary to the existence of the real Shiki
and vice versa: at a certain point in his life, when he could no longer
leave his bed, Shiki's life ceased to exist except in and through words;
here, the literature and the life became one and indistinguishable.

Although this book is the first critical biography of Shiki in English,
I have been preceded by numerous Japanese scholars and am heavily
indebted to them. In matters that are beyond dispute, such as the
factual details of Shiki's life, I have not felt it necessary to give specific
attribution. Where I am indebted for interpretations, this is so
indicated either in note or in text. Unless otherwise indicated, however,
I am responsible for all interpretations of Shiki's poems, ideas, and
broader matters.

Some of my main points concern areas that have not been, to my
knowledge, explored by Japanese scholars. For example, in Chapters 4
and 5, I try to place Shiki's diaries within the context of traditional
literature, particularly the poetic diary[2] and classical haiku prose. I
also trace, in Chapter 3, a common theme in the haiku, tanka, and
prose of Shiki's last years. Again, at least one example of the duality of

consciousness which I feel is central to Shiki, will be found in every chapter.

In general, the view of Shiki presented here seems to me quite different from that of any Japanese work, although I do not think that its outlines, at least, would provoke disagreement. There are, however, three exceptions, major points on which I find myself at odds with accepted critical opinion.

First, the common assertion that Shiki believed Matsuo Bashō to be an inferior poet is, it seems to me, an exaggeration. It is true that in one work Shiki dismissed nine-tenths of Bashō's poems as doggerel; but at the same time he maintained that the excellence of the other tenth was enough to justify Bashō's reputation as a great poet. In other works he went out of his way to assert that Bashō and Buson were equally excellent poets, praising Bashō for his realism and acknowledging the formative influence that Bashō's poetry had had on him. Shiki was not an opponent of Bashō but of Bashō worshipers and the commercialization of the haiku associated with them. The fact that he tried to point out that not every poem Bashō wrote was marked for eternity should not be taken as evidence that he thought Bashō was a hack.

Second, as a critic, Shiki's main contribution is usually assumed to be the idea of the sketch from life. I think his allegiance to it, however, even as a theory, was ambiguous. It seems to me that his indisputable contribution and, from the standpoint of the history of ideas, his more original one, was to insist on the potential of the haiku and tanka as serious literature on a par with the novel and the drama—for when Shiki began his career in the late 1880s the traditional forms of Japanese poetry were regarded as frivolous pastimes incapable of expressing the complexities of modern human beings.

Third, as a poet, essayist, and diarist, Shiki's style is usually described as objective and realistic. In his best writings, however, I find a large lyric and personal element as well. The combination of realism and lyricism, plus an assumption of closeness to the reader, creates Shiki's distinctive tone, it seems to me. In the poetry and prose of his last years, Shiki created a literary persona, a semifictive "I"—in effect, a literary character—and thus showed that traditional forms (haiku, tanka, the diary) could have the psychological complexity demanded of modern literature. Shiki did what it was thought (by late-nineteenth-century critics, including himself) the haiku and the tanka could not do: he made them express individuality. It was not, that is, his seemingly objective description which made his writing modern, but rather his depiction of his own character, of himself.

Shiki's lyricism, at least in the haiku, began to be discussed by Japanese critics for the first time just as I was completing the manuscript of this book in late 1978. In fact it seems, perhaps due to the publication of a new *Complete Works of Shiki* in 1975–1978, that there may be a reassessment of Shiki.[3]

All the translations of poems (except for one, so noted) are my own. Making them gave me more trouble than anything else in the book. So often poems that read perfectly well, even superbly, in the Japanese were reduced to mashed potato in English. In the end, hoping to salvage what could be salvaged, I ignored considerations of consistency. Capitalization, as a rule, I dispensed with, feeling it inappropriate to both the haiku and the tanka; but sometimes I did retain it because the poem seemed to work better with it. Varying such elements may give some sense of otherwise untranslatable stylistic differences as well.

Certain works are mentioned in the text or notes but not in the bibliography because they are not related directly to Shiki and space for the bibliography was limited. For such works, I have given complete bibliographical information in either text or notes. If, however, a work is listed in the bibliography, its complete bibliographical information will only be found there and references within the text or notes give only author, title, city, date of publication, and page number.

Direct quotations from Shiki's works are followed by parentheses, with the volume and page number of the quotation in the Kōdansha edition of Shiki's complete works (see bibliography).

Janine Beichman

University of Library and Information Science

Acknowledgments

This book is an outgrowth of my doctoral dissertation on Shiki, which in turn developed from my master's essay on his diary *A Drop of Ink*. Both were written at the suggestion and under the guidance of Donald Keene. By a combination of dedicated teaching and his own example as a scholar and translator, Donald Keene has nurtured a generation of specialists in Japanese literature. It is a pleasure to record here my continuing debt to him.

Takagi Kiyoko helped me with my first reading of *A Drop of Ink* at Columbia University in 1966–1967. In 1969, when I came to Tokyo, she introduced me to the Wind of the Universe Tanka Society (*Uchūfū Tanka Kai*). Here, writing tanka in an atmosphere at once critical and supportive, I began to understand some of the problems involved in the tanka form in a way that would have been otherwise impossible.

I was also fortunate enough to be allowed to participate in several meetings of the Tokyo University Haiku Society (*Tōdai Haiku Kai*), which is descended from Shiki's original haiku group, the *Hototogisu Kai*, thanks to the kindness of one of its members, Osada Tetsuo.

I am also grateful to the United States government for support provided by several NDFL Fellowships between 1965 and 1968 and a Fullbright-Hays Fellowship in 1970–1971. And to the following people: Konishi Jinichi, Miyoshi Yukio, and Teruoka Yasutaka, for sharing their knowledge with me and telling me their reactions to my ideas. Richard Bowring, Karen Brazell, Margaret Benton Fukasawa, Doris Modry Jason, Kathryn Sparling, Roy Teele and Yamamoto Takeo, for reading and commenting on the manuscript in whole or in part at various stages of its existence. Wada Shigeki and the staff of the Kōdansha *Shiki Zenshū*, especially Izumi Yoshie, for their generous cooperation in providing me with materials and information. Louise Picon Shimizu, for typing most of the manuscript and making many helpful suggestions on vital details of style. Ishizuka Kazumi, for checking the references with meticulous care and, with Ishizuka Hidehiro, compiling the index. And Yagyū Shirō, for kindly correcting the readings for all the haiku and tanka for this paperback edition.

Chronology

1867   Masaoka Shiki born in Matsuyama, Iyo Province (now Ehime Prefecture).

1870   His younger sister Ritsu born.

1872   His father's death. His maternal uncle becomes the family guardian.

1873   Enters elementary school and begins the study of the Chinese classics under his maternal grandfather, Ōhara Kanzan, and calligraphy under an uncle.

1875   Ōhara dies. Shiki's Chinese studies continue under a series of tutors.

1878   Writes "On Western Dogs," an essay for school, and his earliest extant prose. Writes his first poem in Chinese.

1880   Enters Matsuyama Middle School.

1881   Decides to become a politician.

1882   Composes his first tanka.

1883   Withdraws from Matsuyama Middle School and goes to Tokyo. Enters Kyōritsu School.

1884   Passes entrance exam of University Preparatory School (later Higher Middle School). In summer studies English. Begins *Scribblings*.

1885   Fails his examinations. Acquires interest in philosophy.

1888   Becomes enamored of baseball. Becomes interested in aesthetics. Reads Spencer's *On Style*.

1889   Writes *The Origin and Development of Poetry* as essay for school.

1890 Graduates from Higher Middle School. Enters Japanese literature department of Tokyo University, then called Imperial University (*Teikoku Daigaku*).

1891 Skips final examinations in the spring. In winter, begins *The Capital By Moonlight* and *Classified Collection of Haiku*. Loses interest in philosophy. Tries to record real scenes in poetry but is unsuccessful until Bashō's *Monkey's Cloak* opens his eyes.

1892 Shows *The Capital By Moonlight* to Kōda Rohan, who is discouraging. *Talks on Haiku from the Otter's Den* serialized in *Nippon*, and Shiki's haiku reform begins. Withdraws from university. Becomes haiku editor of *Nippon*.

1893 *Indiscriminate Attacks on the Literary World* and *Some Remarks on Bashō* serialized in *Nippon*.

1895 In China as correspondent for *Nippon* during Sino-Japanese War. Meets Mori Ōgai. On return trip, has lung hemorrhage. Hospitalized in Kōbe; nearly dies. Stays with Natsume Sōseki in Matsuyama to convalesce and while there leads a group of young haiku poets for whom he writes *The Elements of Haiku*, serializing it in *Nippon*.

1896 Reads Buson's *Shin Hanatsumi* [New Flower Picking].

1897 *Hototogisu*, magazine of the Nippon school of haiku, begins publication in Matsuyama. *The Haiku World of 1896* and *The Haiku Poet Buson* serialized in *Nippon*. Undergoes surgery for complications of tuberculosis.

1898 Series of lecture-discussions on Buson at Shiki's home. *Letters to a Tanka Poet* serialized in *Nippon*; begins tanka reform. Meetings of Negishi Tanka Society begin at his home. *Hototogisu* place of publication moves to Tokyo and it becomes a general magazine of the arts. *Record of the Little Garden* published in *Hototogisu*; prose movement begins.

1900 His essay *Realistic Prose* serialized in *Nippon*. Begins society for the study of the *Manyōshū*.

1901   *A Drop of Ink* serialized in *Nippon*. Mountain Society for study of sketch from life prose meets at his house from time to time. Writes *Stray Notes While Lying on My Back*.

1902   Publishes Volume One of *Selections from the Haiku Notebook of the Otter's Den*. *A Sixfoot Sickbed* serialized in *Nippon*. Dies at home in early autumn after first setting down in his own hand his three last haiku.

Chapter One
Life: From Samurai to Poet

Photographs of Masaoka Shiki reveal a symmetrical face, with rather square jaw and forehead, and widely spaced eyes. The overall impression is one of balance and strength, even in the photographs of his last years, when he was an invalid.

The impression the photographs give is an accurate one, for Shiki was a man of great energy and vision with the charisma necessary to inspire and propel a literary movement even as a bedridden invalid. In personality, he was deeply ambitious, taking his chosen vocation—literature—with great seriousness. Yet, at the same time, he was witty, ironic, even, at times, frivolous. As a friend, he could be aggressively domineering or touchingly protective. A passionate man, with fierce attachments to his friends, he never, so far as is known, had a romantic involvement; his primary physical enjoyment, particularly after he became an invalid, appears to have been food. As a writer, some time may be required before one acquires a taste for him, but once one does, he never palls; an irresistible sense of life and animation imbues his works.

Shiki's life lends itself to metaphor. From his birth until his choice of a vocation in 1892, it can be seen as a journey through different cultural worlds, moving from the sober Tokugawa period Confucianism of his early upbringing into the heady, exciting atmosphere of the early Meiji period, with its many new literary, intellectual, and political currents imported from the West. Finally, in choosing literature as his vocation, he settled at first on a part of it—the haiku—which represented for him both the values of the (previous) Tokugawa period and those of the (current) Meiji period. His ambition for immortality through literature at first knew no bounds. But in the end, his health destroyed by tuberculosis, he made peace

1

with his own mortality, and in his last poems expressed a sense of spiritual resignation that seems close to enlightenment.

In light of Shiki's spiritual and intellectual journey from the world of the Tokugawa period into that of the Meiji period and then finally to a kind of synthesis of the two, it seems particularly appropriate that he was born in 1867, just one year before the Meiji Restoration, in the last year of the Tokugawa period.

Matsuyama: From Confucianism to Civil Rights (1867–1883)

Shiki was born on October 14, 1867, into a low-ranking samurai family in the castle town of Matsuyama han on the island of Shikoku. His father, a man of undistinguished attainments, was an alcoholic and died when Shiki was five. The family had not been well off even before the death of Shiki's father; but with his death and the commutation of samurai pensions into a lump-sum payment in money by the new government, they, like most of the other samurai families in Matsuyama, were left with no fixed source of income. Shiki's mother was forced to teach sewing in order to support him and his younger sister Ritsu. In such an environment, education was the only form of wealth; it seems natural that Shiki's maternal grandfather, Ōhara Kanzan, who was a distinguished Confucian scholar and Shiki's earliest teacher, became Shiki's ideal.

Kanzan was a samurai's samurai: he possessed fortitude, pride, a contempt for material wealth, and a detached humor that enabled him to endure the most humiliating poverty with equanimity. Nothing could better evoke the character of such a man, and the lineage as well of many of Shiki's later attitudes, than the following anecdote, told by Kanzan's son (Shiki's uncle), Katō Tsunetada:

I think it was the end of 1873—one day while I was massaging my father's back, Kinbei, the owner of the Tanakaya pawn shop on Tōjin Street, strode in without even knocking, and said, "Sensei, let's have the interest you owe me."

My father, with an air of slight embarrassment, replied, "Kinbei, I'm terribly sorry, but this year we haven't been able to make the New Year's rice cakes yet, and I haven't even money to buy the childrens' kites. I'll definitely repay part after the New Year, so please have just a little more patience."

Kinbei was silent for some time. Then he suddenly stood up, threw the water from the handwashing basin into the garden, and said, "Your kites and rice cakes are no concern of mine. At least I can take this." And he walked out carrying the brass basin, which was over two feet in diameter.

My father turned to my mother and said with a laugh, "Kinbei always was a man of action, wasn't he!"

My mother went silently to the storeroom and wept by herself. Soon afterwards my younger brother came in from playing, and entreated my father, "Papa, when are you going to buy our kites?"

I still can't forget how bad the rice cakes in our soup tasted the next morning. I resolved then and there to cheer my father up by redeeming the hand basin at all costs. During the day, I pounded rice and in the evenings I copied out an elementary school text called *Vocabulary*. After a few months, I proudly brought home the basin from the Tanakaya. My father looked at me with annoyance, and said sternly, "Do you suppose you'll become great by worrying about such trivial things?"[1]

Kanzan was adamantly opposed to the new world of the Meiji period. He refused, for example, to study any Western languages. In the last line of a Chinese poem which he had Shiki copy out, he expressed his disgust for languages which were written horizontally instead of, like Japanese, vertically: "Never in your life read that writing which sidles sideways like a crab across the page."

He also clung to the outward signs of his samurai identity as long as possible. In 1871, the government had authorized former samurai to cut their hair and discard their swords. Kanzan not only refused to do either but even made Shiki follow his example. His efforts to resist the tide of change proved futile, however. Shiki, having become the only boy (except for his cousin Ryō, also under Kanzan's tutelage) at school with long hair, repeatedly begged permission to cut his hair and finally won the support of his uncle, who asked Kanzan if he would not change his mind. Realizing that further resistance was useless, Kanzan reluctantly gave his permission, and Shiki joyfully cut his hair. Until 1876, when the government went one step further and forbade former samurai to wear swords, Shiki was never permitted to go visiting without a short sword or dagger at his waist.

Although Shiki entered public elementary school at age six, the real center of his education, at least until he was in his teens, was outside the public schools, in his studies of classical Chinese history, philosophy, and literature under a series of private tutors. The first of these tutors was his grandfather Kanzan, from whom he learned the elements of reading Chinese beginning in 1874. Each morning he arose at five, when it was still dark, and sleepily made his way to his grandfather's house. There he studied the *Mencius,* one of the so-called "Five Classics," proceeding later in the morning to the public elementary school.

Kanzan doted on his grandson and said it was a pleasure to teach him, for he never forgot anything. Shiki in turn acquired from him a reverence for scholarship which he carried with him for the rest of his life and which deeply influenced his approach to literature. He preserved this even after he had discarded much else of the Confucian philosophy and samurai morality that Kanzan had tried to instill in him. Unlike his doting grandfather, however, Shiki did not remember himself as a diligent student. In *Fude Makase* [Scribblings], a series of short, miscellaneous essays he wrote between 1884 and 1892, he confessed to having been an indifferent student who wanted the glory of being an eminent scholar but was really more interested in writing poetry than in studying:

As a boy, I was too lazy to study. When I was seven or eight, Kanzan reproached me. "When I was a boy," he said, "I did not play all the time as you do."

This made me think. He was the foremost Confucian scholar in Matsuyama han. Being a constant witness to the respect he was shown in all quarters, I too wanted to become a scholar, to be his equal. But his words made me realize that he had devoted himself to learning from childhood. This touched something in me, and I said to myself, "I want to surpass him. But if he has always studied so hard I'll never be able to become his assistant, let alone his superior. Still, I don't like to study. What can I do?"

Time passed but my thoughts did not change; even after I had come to Tokyo, I was the same. The only thing I studied at all was writing poetry; school work always came last. However, Kanzan's admonition remained firmly in my mind, and I always thought I should be studying, even though I hated school. (X, 111–12)

Kanzan died in the spring of 1875, at age fifty-seven, while gazing at the cherry-blossoms in his garden. After his death, Shiki continued his studies under other teachers. By the time he was eleven, he had composed his first poem in classical Chinese, and was also able to compose essays in that language.

Most of the texts he read under his tutors had been written in ancient China and were typical of those that had been used by young men of the samurai class during the late Tokugawa period. The contents of the essays he wrote for public school, however, were a far cry from those of the Chinese classics. When he was thirteen, he collected several of these essays for his own amusement. The first piece in the collection, *Yōken Setsu* [On Western Dogs], is Shiki's earliest extant piece of writing:

Western dogs are the best of animals and often do what people cannot. Let me explain. Japanese dogs only help in hunting, and scare away burglars at night. However, Western dogs save people from drowning, and rescue travelers buried under heavy snow in cold countries. People use them to pull sleds and deliver letters. I have not room to enumerate their virtues. How much superior, then, are Western dogs to Japanese dogs! The virtues of Western dogs are truly great." (IX, 14–15)

As a child, Shiki had shed with great relief the long hair that was a badge of his samurai birth and a symbolic link with the past. Now, approaching adolescence, he showed himself open to Western civilization in a way that directly contradicted Kanzan's adamant resistance.

Throughout his eleventh and twelfth years, Shiki's interests continued to expand to include matters forbidden by the stern Confucianism of his grandfather, and his life became correspondingly more lively. He and several other boys shared a tutor for mathematics and reading, who, finding both himself and his students too tired for serious study at their evening meetings, would instead spend most of their lessons recounting the plots of popular Chinese and Japanese novels of adventure. The boys soon discovered that they could borrow such works from a rental library by themselves. But Shiki's mother, in accord with the then common view of novels as worthless at best and scandalous at worst, at first forbade him to read anything but his

schoolbooks and the Chinese classics. She lifted this prohibition when
he was fourteen or fifteen, and he devoured the works of Takizawa
Bakin (1767–1848), the leading novelist of the late Tokugawa
period, as well as such famous Chinese novels of adventure as *San-kuo-chih yen-i* [The Romance of the Three Kingdoms], *Hsi yu chi*
[Record of a Journey to the West], and *Shui hu chuan* [Water
Margin]. He also was able to borrow several medieval Japanese war
epics from a friend, including the *Gempei Seisuiki* [Annals of the Rise
and Fall of the Minamoto and the Taira], the *Hōgen Monogatari*
[Tale of the Hōgen], and the *Heiji Monogatari* [Tale of the Taira
Clan]. As his handwriting was excellent, he enjoyed copying out well-
known or especially moving passages, and in time amassed a great
many of them.

At the same time, he also won permission to go hear professional
storytellers recite their traditional tales of war and military valor.
These, together with the adventure stories of his teacher and the
novels and tales he borrowed from the library and his friends, were for
a time his great passions.

The new world thus opened up for him did not, however, eclipse
his enthusiasm for more traditional study. In 1880, he and a group of
friends had formed a group which came to be called the Poetry
Lovers' Society [*Dōshin Ginsha*] and it continued to occupy a great
deal of his time until 1882. The group had originally been formed
when Shiki and four others did so well in their examinations at middle
school that each received a work by the eminent Tokugawa Confucian
historian Rai Sanyō (1780–1832). Unable to read it by themselves,
they turned to the father of one of them, a Confucian scholar of the
Chu Hsi school, and he agreed to tutor them in it. From there, they
went on to study the writings of the T'ang and Sung periods and the
philosophical works of Chu Hsi. Then they began to compose Chinese
poetry, meeting once a week at each other's homes to discuss their
efforts.

The five friends often climbed the dike by the river on the outskirts
of Matsuyama and declaimed poetry to the stars, or discoursed on the
philosophy of Chu Hsi while gazing at the river. Another of their
favorite gathering-places was a study-library of three mats that was
added on to the Masaoka home around this time. Since Shiki's mother

taught sewing, the living room had always been taken up with her work until then and there had been very little space for her son's activities. In Shiki's new room, he put a desk and bookcase in one corner, while papers and books soon crammed the rest of the area until there was barely room to step. In spite of the clutter, members of the Poetry Lovers' Society became frequent visitors, and it was from there that their circulating magazines were edited and distributed.

Sometimes the magazines had contributions by all the members; sometimes Shiki had to write an entire issue by himself. In either case, the contents consisted of essays, travel accounts, and Chinese poetry. The members would write comments and criticism in the margins as the sole copy circulated, and this often led to lively debate. Shiki's little room became the literary salon for five young authors and he, though two years younger than the rest, became their mentor—as later his home in Tokyo became the locale for meetings where the eager and aspiring haiku and tanka poets who wrote and discussed poetry decided the course of the modern haiku and tanka.

It was a happy time. As Shiki's cousin and youthful companion Minami Ryō later reminisced, "In those days we were free. We were not overseen by the school authorities or the police. If we wanted to go somewhere—to the mountains, a river, or a play—we did; and we read anything we pleased."

This idyllic life ended in 1882, when Shiki's interests broadened to include politics and political debate. The power of the peoples' rights movement, brought to Matsuyama in 1874, had become somewhat attenuated by 1881, but the political martyrs it had made—including Kusama Jifuku, a former principal of Matsuyama Middle School, which Shiki attended from 1880—had made a deep impression on Shiki. Then in 1882, there was a revival of its forces, and Shiki became a political enthusiast. Whenever possible, he and his friends attended the meetings of the Prefectural Assembly and political rallies, even if it meant playing truant. They formed several public-speaking clubs under the sponsorship of the school, and tried to use them as a forum for radical opinions. The new principal, however, was a conservative installed by a government bent on crushing the peoples' rights movement. While he encouraged the formation of clubs for debating and public speaking, he tried to suppress the expression of any radical political ideas. Shiki, whose sympathies were completely with the peoples' rights movement, naturally came into conflict with him, and finally was banned from speaking entirely.

At this time, Shiki shared two dreams with his cousin Ryō: one was to become political martyrs like the former principal of their school, while the other was to go live in some remote mountain fastness, away from all human strife. The incongruity illustrates the essence of this period in Shiki's life, when so many possibilities seemed his. As Ryō later wrote, "We reached adolescence just after the dissolution of the feudal system. All had been sown afresh. But while the old order had fallen, nothing new had yet been created in its place."

It was up to Shiki to decide what he would be—there was no path laid out for him to follow as there might have been had he been born a generation earlier. His freedom was held in check, however, by two factors—first, the scruples given him by his Confucian upbringing, and second, his poverty. The following reminiscence speaks of the inner barrier which kept him from considering literature as a profession, although it appealed to him more than anything else:

I liked writing best. But I was under the influence of Chinese studies then, and thought I should not let poetry or painting become the whole object of my life. And yet, nothing else appealed to me. I detested medicine. And of course I despised science. Rather than either, I thought I would go into law or politics, and told people that I had decided on my career. . . . (X, 40)

Then there was his poverty, common to most of the descendants of the lower samurai class in this period. Their principal occupation before had been the teaching and study of the martial arts. But now no one was interested in either. Nor did they have the security of their former yearly stipends from the daimyo.

To Shiki, Tokyo seemed salvation. In one of the speeches made at a public-speaking club, he had urged any young man of ambition to go to Tokyo, describing it as a great city, where one might "mix with people from all the countries of the world, with wise and sagacious men, and receive their teachings" (IX, 118). With that longing to be reborn that so often fills people as they stand on the border between childhood and adolescence and look into their future, Shiki saw Tokyo as a new world, the whole world, of which he had as yet known but a tiny part. He could not wait to leap into his own future. Later he wrote of this time, "For several months . . . [m]y desire to go to Tokyo to study gave me no peace. I felt that if the chance came, I would even run away" (X, 46).

Shiki's cousin Ryō had left for Tokyo in 1882, and in the following year one friend after another was rumored to be going. Shiki wrote that if one so much as caught a cold and was absent from school for a few days, it was assumed that he had left for Tokyo. But Shiki had little hope for himself. His maternal uncle and legal guardian Ōhara Tsunenori opposed his going, as did the maternal uncle to whom he looked for support in Tokyo, Katō Tsunetada. Their reasons, however, seem to have been financial rather than theoretical: as soon as Katō heard that the former daimyo of Matsuyama han had established a scholarship for boys of samurai descent and that Shiki, an excellent student, had a good chance of winning one if he were in Tokyo, he wrote his nephew urging him to come at once.

Katō's letter arrived on June 8, 1883. On the ninth, Shiki's mother, Yae, stayed up all night sewing her son a new traveling kimono, while Shiki made a final speech to his fellow students at a public-speaking club. The next day, he left by boat, seen off by relatives and a few friends. Yet his eagerness for the future was tempered by regret for the past: he later wrote that the moment when the ship pulled out of the harbor was one of the saddest in his life.

Tokyo: From Politics to Philosophy to Literature (1883–1889)

In Tokyo, after an initial period of settling in, Shiki entered the Kyōritsu Middle School. The usual process was to complete the three-year course there and then, if one wished to go on, enter a university preparatory school. Shiki, however, took the examination for Daigaku Yobimon (University Preparatory School), which was affiliated with Teikoku Daigaku (Imperial University, later incorporated into the present Tokyo University) while still in his second year and, much to his surprise, passed it.

He later wrote in the journal *Bokujū Itteki* [A Drop of Ink, 1901] that he had taken the examination without studying for it beforehand and merely "for the fun of it"; his main motive was to keep several classmates who were taking it for the experience company. When he discovered that of the five or six who had taken it, he was one of the two who had passed, he was astonished. "I decided," he wrote, "that passing examinations was as easy as farting" (XI, 210).

When Shiki came to Tokyo, he had been intent on politics or law as a career. But the year after entering University Preparatory School, in the spring of 1885, he decided to become a philosopher instead. The decision was occasioned largely by his uncle Katō Tsunetada. In *Scribblings,* Shiki recalled:

Once my uncle took us to a secluded farm house. . . . After talking of this and that, he turned to me and said, "It's really remarkable how a piece of white paper will turn black when you spill India ink on it. And when a man puts on a woman's clothes and does his hair up like a woman, he looks just like a woman. But still, a man is a man; one can never say he is a woman."

How happy I was when I heard him talk like that! Three years of study seemed worthless compared to that conversation. But I still did not know about philosophy. . . . After that I entered the Kyōritsu School and studied the *Chuang Tzu.*[2] It was the most fascinating book I had ever read and it delighted me; but even then I still did not know that philosophy existed. I'm not sure how I finally did learn, but in the spring of 1885, I set my sights on philosophy and resolved that no one would deflect me from my goal. (X, 39–40)

For all his enthusiasm, however, Shiki learned nothing about philosophy beyond what his uncle and the *Chuang Tzu* had taught him. In the essay *Jūnen Mae no Natsu* [A Summer Ten Years Ago, 1898], he described his combined ignorance and ambition as of 1888 in his usual pithy, humorous style: "Now I thought I wanted to be a great philosopher, though I knew nothing about philosophy. The sum total of my knowledge of it lay in the simple definition of philosophy as the supreme study and philosophers as the greatest of men (including prime ministers)" (XII, 226). He still did not know of any other Western philosopher besides Herbert Spencer,[3] and was never to read more of Spencer's works than *Philosophy of Style* and an exposition of Spencer's philosophy in Japanese called *Kagaku no Genri* [Principles of Science]. His decision to become a philosopher did not make him study any harder than before, either. In fact, he failed his final examinations at University Preparatory School in 1885.

Sometime later, his ambition shifted to aesthetics. He described this process, too, in *Scribblings*:

Although I intended to study philosophy, I had a passion for poetry and felt I could not live without novels. It struck me as strange: how could I like two such completely opposing and incompatible things as philosophy and literature at the same time? (The reasons I thought them opposed were that philosophers were serious men, not concerned with the trivia of literature; Buddhist priests did not write novels; and I had not yet discovered that Spencer wrote poetry.) I found it odd. But I could not decide on one over the other, so I declared that philosophy would be my vocation and poetry my avocation. Meanwhile I kept asking myself how the two were related. Sometime later, I learned of the existence of aesthetics. The realization that one could discuss such arts as literature and painting in philosophical terms made me so happy I all but jumped for joy. Finally, I changed my aim to aesthetics. (X, 41–42)

Shiki's excitement when he first discovered aesthetics did not arise from its content or the light it shed on art; if it had, he would have read something about aesthetics, but he never did. His excitement came from the fact that aesthetics was a part of scholarly learning and yet, at the same time, included literature, thereby reconciling two spheres—the intellectual and the artistic—which he had thought were mutually exclusive.

Shiki's belief that these two spheres were mutually exclusive came from his Confucian education: in the Confucian hierarchy of values, literature and the arts occupied a relatively low place among human activities—they were esteemed as accomplishments, but were put below the "serious" occupations of scholarship (*gakumon*) and the art of government. Shiki had accepted this hierarchy; that is why he had felt it impossible to say he wanted to become a writer or a painter and had instead declared he wished to be a lawyer or a politician. The lawyer or politician was, of course, involved with the art of government; Shiki's next ambition, to be a philosopher, symbolized the sphere of scholarship. Yet, all during the period when he was avowing these ambitions, he was still in love with literature. When he discovered aesthetics, it must have seemed to offer a way to legitimize the pursuit of literature, for it applied scholarship to literature.

In short, Shiki needed to know no more about aesthetics except that it existed in order to be liberated from the scruples that had kept him from conceiving of literature as a vocation. It is not surprising, then, that his diligence in studying aesthetics never matched his initial enthusiasm; in fact, there is no record that he ever read through a single work on the subject.[4]

He was reading widely in contemporary literature, however. In doing so, he encountered a new development in the history of thought: the conception of literature as a unity embracing many genres. This, too, must have aided his effort to find an intellectual justification for literature. In the early to mid-1880s, a new conception of literature was enunciated which broke with the Tokugawa period Confucian view of literature as either didactic or entertaining, for it insisted that literature was a method of expressing truth that needed no justification beyond itself.

During the Tokugawa period (1603–1867) there had existed no word that could translate the modern English "literature," as a term to collectively denote any kind of poem, novel, short story, essay, drama, or sometimes even history and biography. Furthermore, there was no form of literature which was considered to have an intrinsic value in itself, as a means of expressing truth. A literary work only had value, in the Confucian hierarchy, when it expressed a moral or philosophical truth—in other words, when it was didactic. This belief gave rise to the doctrine of "encourage virtue and reprove vice" (*kanzen chōaku*) as the Confucian formula for the role of literature in society. Works which did not do this had no value at all, but were merely entertainment or diversion.

Different literary forms were associated with different classes and this, too, affected their valuation. The haiku, for example, was associated with the merchant class by the late Tokugawa period, while the tanka retained an association with the nobility. The distinctions which grew up between these genres on the basis of such seemingly superficial differences as their class associations, the subjects and diction suitable to them, and their rules of composition, tended to obscure their underlying common nature as poetry. A tanka poet, for example, would identify him or herself not as a poet, but as a tanka-person (*kajin*), while a haiku poet would refer to him or herself as a haiku-person (*haijin*). The two would feel their genres to be mutually exclusive; a haiku poet would not dream of seriously composing tanka, nor would a tanka poet trespass within the bounds of haiku except in play. The aesthetic standards, the terms of analysis, the aims of each were felt to be totally different.

It was not until 1885 that the conception of literature as a unity embracing many genres, all of which were potentially modes of expressing truth, was first introduced in the modern period.[5] The critic and novelist Tsubouchi Shōyō (1859–1935), who had become acquainted with it through his readings of British novelists and critics, introduced it in his critical work *Shōsetsu Shinzui* [The Essence of the Novel, 1885–1886]. Shōyō postulated almost all genres (but principally the novel and the drama) as one distinct category of culture and maintained that this category, literature (*bungaku*), had an intrinsic value in itself, which lay largely in its ability to convey accurately the real feelings of real human beings. Implied in his view was the worth of literature, especially fiction and drama, as a vocation suitable for the traditional Confucian gentleman-intellectual. This view was shocking to many at the time because of the unsavory associations of the Tokugawa period novel (*gesaku*). Skiki's mother, who, it will be remembered, had forbidden Shiki to read such works until he was in his teens, was typical; and in the early nineteenth century, some novelists had even been arrested as threats to public order and morality. In *Scribblings*'s brief essay "Nihon no Shōsetsu" [The Japanese Novel], Shiki vividly described the effect that Shōyō had:

Harunoya Oboro [Shōyō's pen name] burst upon the literary scene asserting that the novel was an art and not to be held in contempt. In fact novelists until now, especially Bakin, have despised the novel themselves. Thus, I think, they sought a rationalization in the doctrine of "reward virtue, chastise vice" [*kanzen chōaku*]. In their heart of hearts, they did not despise the novel; it was only that they had no way to win respect for it, and were unable to discover a reason for honoring it. Since Harunoya Oboro destroyed this illusion, ardent men of talent everywhere have all begun to flourish their brushes in public and achieve greatness in the novel.

Shōyō, however, explicitly excluded the haiku and the tanka from his definition of literature, asserting that they were to short to express the complex feelings of modern human beings. In this, he was only expressing the commonly held view of the time that Japan's traditional poetic forms were unsuitable for the new age. This view had also been expressed by the authors of *Shintaishi Shō* [Collection of New-Style Verse, 1882], the first collection of free verse and translated Western verse in Japanese, which Shiki also read. Shiki himself shared the opinion for a time. In an essay he wrote in 1889, however, *Shiika no Kigen oyobi Hensen* [The Origin and Development of Poetry], he utilized an idea from Spencer's *Philosophy of Style* to defend the haiku from its many contemporary detractors.

Spencer had written, "The shortest sentence is the best" and related this to "the economy of the mental energies." In other words, the shorter and simpler a sentence, the less energy was used up by the reader in making it out, and the more energy was left for absorbing its meaning. Shiki, somewhat distorting Spencer's argument, took this to imply that the shorter a poetic form was, the deeper the meaning it could evoke. This meant, paradoxically, that the more complex human thoughts and emotions became, the more suitable they would be for the haiku. He concluded, "Which has more to offer, the scant seventeen syllables of Bashō's poem on the old pond, with their layers of meaning—or Hitomaro's tanka on the long, trailing tail of the mountain bird, which expresses but one meaning?"[6]

The implication of Shiki's position in this essay went beyond the relative merits of short and long poetic forms and opposition to the prevailing low opinion of the haiku. By extension, he was declaring his independence from the Confucian teaching that deep meaning could best be expressed in philosophical essays or in Chinese poems (longer than the haiku and tanka), and thus taking one more step away from the teachings of Kanzan and his Confucian heritage.

In the spring of the same year he wrote *The Origin and Development of Poetry,* Shiki coughed blood for the second time (the first had been the previous summer), one of the early signs of the tuberculosis that would tragically shorten his life. The following year, he graduated from Kōtō Chūgakkō (Higher Middle School, the new name for University Preparatory School), and entered the Japanese literature department of Imperial University (predecessor of the present Tokyo University.)

Literature as a Vocation: Year of Decision (1892)

While Shiki was grappling with the problem of how to justify the practice of the haiku in terms that would satisfy both the intellectual prejudices of the late Tokugawa period and those of the early Meiji period, he was also steadily writing haiku as an avocation. He had begun to write haiku sometime after he came to Tokyo, in 1884 or 1885. When he returned to Matsuyama for the second time, in the summer of 1886, he bore an introduction to a now forgotten haiku poet called Ōhara Kijū, and went with his friend Yanagihara Kyokudō (1867–1957), later one of his disciples, to call on him. Kijū had been a disciple of Sakurai Baishitsu (1769–1852), considered one of the three great haiku masters of the Tempō era (1830–1843), and was over eighty years old at the time. His study was papered all over— ceiling, walls, and doors—with haiku and drawings. While Kyokudō was admiring the ceiling, Shiki showed Kijū some haiku he had written. Kijū praised them and by way of reply composed two haiku for Shiki about a dragon bounding over Mt. Fuji. The mention of the dragon, of course, was meant to suggest Kijū's conviction that Shiki would become a great poet. It must have been immensely encouraging. Although this was to be their only meeting, Shiki later wrote that Kijū had been his only teacher of haiku.

Shiki's fascination with the haiku and other forms of literature continued to grow stronger. Eventually he became so carried away that he stopped attending university classes. He left the dormitory in Hongō where he had been living as a scholarship student, and rented a house in Komagome. He later wrote of this time:

[The house] was in a very quiet spot, suited to studying; but the only studying I did was of haiku and novels. When I had an examination, I would begin to prepare a few days before by putting away all the haiku books on my desk and then placing there only the notes necessary for the examination. My desk was usually in a state of total disorder, so when I sat down quietly and saw it so bare and neat, I felt an indefinable pleasure. As soon as I felt so pleasant and cheerful, a haiku would flash into my mind. When I opened my notebook, a seventeen syllable verse would emerge before I could read a page.

I couldn't write it down since I had put my poetry notebook and even my writing paper away. So I would write it on the lampshade. Verse after verse came forth. Entranced, I abandoned the examination to cover the lampshade with writing. . . .

I was in such a state that as soon as I tried to stop writing haiku and prepare for an examination, verses would flash through my mind in droves. Examinations came to mean nothing but a surge of poetry. Bewitched by the goddess of haiku, nothing could save me. I failed the final examinations of 1892 . . . [and] withdrew from school once and for all. (XI, 214–15)

Shiki regarded his academic failure with a mixture of nonchalance and relief. In the middle of a letter made up largely of haiku (to his friend and later disciple Iogi Hyōtei, 1870–1937), he added casually:

You must have heard—I've finally received the honor of failing.

> minazuki no   In the coolness
> kokū ni suzushi   of the empty sixth-month sky . . .
> hototogisu   the cuckoo's cry.

At the thought that it resembled a death-bed poem, I burst out laughing. (XVIII, 327)

Shiki's indifference to academic achievement and his earlier espousal of radical politics may make him seem something of an anti-Establishment figure; but beneath it all, he retained many traditional samurai attitudes. One was his scorn of material wealth, another his readiness to throw away his life for a good cause. Both were amply illustrated when, having formally withdrawn from university, Shiki had to forfeit as well the scholarship that had sustained him for eight years. At the end of January 1892, he wrote that he had only one sen and six rin left in his pocket, and could not even buy a writing brush. But even in these desperate circumstances, his fortitude would have made Kanzan proud. When his friend (later disciple) Takahama Kyoshi (1874–1959) wrote him saying he would like to become a novelist, but feared he might not be able to earn a living, Shiki's reply was indignant:

So you can't make a living as a novelist—why not try farming or teaching? Or even begging—what difficulties would that present? Were you born into the world to make a living? Or have you another aim, that of becoming a novelist or something akin? If you want to become a novelist but are worried about how you will eat, then let me share my bowl of rice with you (though I am not as well off as I once was). If, in return, you become a great novelist, it will be my greatest joy. . . . I do not presume to urge you to become a novelist. I say only this—be firm of purpose and don't worry about trivialities. And remember the saying: *the final tax you pay to achieve your goal is your life* [emphasis in original]. (XVIII, 239)

1892 was a turning point in Shiki's life. Free now of the necessity to go through the motions of studying for university, he devoted himself to two enterprises: reading through all the haiku written until his own time—this in preparation for *Haiku Bunrui* [Classified Collection of Haiku, 1900]—and working on a novella.

It is necessary to say here that even after his 1889 defense of haiku in *The Origin and Development of Poetry* and his "bewitchment" by "the goddess of haiku" in 1891, Shiki did not foresee his own future as a poet. Of all literary genres, the novel, because of the work of Tsubouchi Shōyō, had been the first to metamorphosize into a vehicle fit to express the new ways of thinking of the Meiji period. Shiki, in common with most of his contemporaries, found the figure of the novelist immensely more appealing than that of the old-fashioned haiku masters. No matter how much he enjoyed writing haiku himself, the profession of haiku master could not have held much appeal.

In 1884, soon after coming to Tokyo, Shiki had read Yano Ryū-kei's *Keikoku Bidan* [A Noble Tale of Statesmanship, 1883], one of the leading political novels of the early Meiji period, and been much taken by it. The following year, he read Shōyō's novel, *Tōsei Shosei Katagi* [Portraits of Contemporary Students, 1885–1886]. He recorded his admiration for both, and especially the latter nearly two decades later in the reminiscence *Tennōji Han no Kagyūro* [The Snail House Near Tennōji, 1902]:

I remember that my surprise and joy when I read it were almost boundless. For I, who had had no idea how many different kinds of novels there might be besides Bakin's novels, Shunsui's tales of passion, or the stereotyped newspaper serials of the time, the novelty of *A Noble Tale of Statesmanship* had been astounding enough; but when I encountered *Portraits of Contemporary Students* there was nothing in it that failed to amaze me, from its use of a combination of the literary and spoken languages [*gazoku-setchū buntai*] to the realism and energy of its plot, and, beyond this, to the fact that, unlike novels up until then, it was not vulgar in spirit but exhibited a kind of good taste.

About Shōyō's critical work, *Shōsetsu Shinzui* [The Essence of the Novel, 1885], Shiki wrote in the same reminiscence:

> In such works as *The Essence of the Novel,* Shōyō expressed as a logical argument what I myself had been thinking; this is why, for children like ourselves who had not yet studied seriously and accordingly had no fixed convictions, his argument and the actual novel taken together were a great inspiration. I came to think, then, that there was no other path for me to take but that sort of novel in that sort of style, and lost myself to it utterly.[7]

In 1890, Shiki read *Fūryū Butsu* [The Romantic Buddha, 1889], by Kōda Rohan, one of the leading authors of the Meiji period. With his typical enthusiasm, he decided it was the greatest story ever written and Rohan the greatest writer in the world. In 1892, he visited Rohan with his own first story, *Tsuki no Miyako* [The Capital by Moonlight, 1892], which he had modeled on *The Romantic Buddha.* Rohan, however, although quite cordial and willing to engage in lively literary debate, did not encourage Shiki's novelistic ambition. This was in March; by May he wrote in a letter to Kyoshi that he no longer wanted to be a novelist, but had decided to become a poet (*shijin*).

Within the general category of "poet," Shiki chose the haiku to begin with—but there is no evidence that he ever intended to limit himself to that form alone. On the contrary, all the evidence points to the conclusion that he always considered himself as either a poet, or a writer in general (*bungakusha*). Still, if he were to engage in the practice of the haiku seriously, it was obvious that he would have to reform the contemporary haiku completely or else follow in the footsteps of the old-fashioned haiku masters he so despised. This involved theoretical and critical writing, then, as well as creative. Work on *Classified Collection of Haiku* had been a sort of preparation for this enterprise, for it had given him an historical overview of the haiku through its primary sources, the poems themselves. The knowledge he gained through this was then incorporated into *Dassai Shooku Haiwa* [Talks on Haiku from the Otter's Den],[8] a series of thirty-eight articles published in the newspaper *Nippon* from June 26 through October 2 of 1892. *Talks on Haiku from the Otter's Den* was Shiki's clarion call for reform of the haiku, directed toward drawing attention to its potential as a serious art form while at the same time attacking the old-fashioned haiku masters whom Shiki held largely responsible for its present degradation.

In November, Shiki had his mother and sister come to Tokyo, for he was now earning enough to be able to support them there. In December, he became the haiku editor of *Nippon*, formalizing an association that was to last until his death. During the next ten years, Shiki published most of his major critical works in *Nippon*, as well as two extraordinary diaries, and many of his over ten thousand haiku and two thousand tanka.

Haiku Reform and Confrontation with Mortality (1893–1897)

In 1893 and the first half of 1894, during negotiations with Britain for the revision of the unequal treaties, the government was under constant attack by a broad-based coalition movement that wanted it to take a more aggressive attitude toward Britain. In 1894, in an effort to quiet the opposition, the government dissolved the Diet twice in six months and forced *Nippon*, which had taken a leading role in the movement, to cease publication temporarily. Kuga Katsunan (1857– 1907), the editor of *Nippon*, thereupon launched a family-style illustrated newspaper, *Shōnippon* [Little Japan], and appointed Shiki as its editor-in-chief. *Shōnippon* survived only six months; in the meantime, *Nippon* had resumed publication, and Shiki returned to his old job there as haiku editor. His association with *Shōnippon* had been crucial, however, for it was through it that he met the Western-style artist Nakamura Fusetsu (1866–1943) and, under his influence, began to clarify still more his ideas on the haiku, borrowing certain concepts of realism from art and wedding these to what he had already received from Shōyō.

Almost simultaneously with Shiki's return to *Nippon*, the Sino-Japanese War broke out (on July 25, 1894), opposition to the government was forgotten, and the nation threw its full support behind the government.

The national mood was one of unmistakable confidence. Shiki shared in the common excitement and wished with all his heart to go to China. In the unfinished autobiographical story *Waga Yamai* [My Sickness, 1900], he recorded his thoughts at the time: "The loneliness at the newspaper's office now [with so many gone as correspondents to China] is really terrible. . . . What point is there in having been born a man unless I can accompany the army?" (XIII, 348–49). When another war correspondent was needed, Shiki volunteered for the job and finally obtained it, although his colleagues and superiors tried to dissuade him because of his poor health.

In 1889, when he coughed blood from the lungs for the first time, Shiki had taken the pen name *Shiki* which is the Sino-Japanese reading for *hototogisu*, usually translated as "cuckoo," the bird that, according to legend, coughs blood as it sings. But this was his only concession to illness. He continued to lead such an active life that by 1894 he had suffered several more lung hemmorhages, and the tuberculosis that would take his life when he was thirty-five had begun its course.

In spite of his condition, Shiki wrote, "I had no fears to hold me back. Of course, I was ready to throw my life away" (XIII, 350). In conversation with a friend shortly before leaving Tokyo, he said, "Naturally, when one leaves for war, one must think of oneself as already dead" (XIII, 351).

Shiki could behave with such recklessness and speak with such samurai panache, only because he possessed a youthful sense of immortality. The realization that he, too, might die struck him for only one brief moment before he left Japan: as the train taking him to Hiroshima (from whence he would sail for China) pulled out of Tokyo, he was assailed for a moment by an unbearable feeling of loneliness:

I had kept saying until then that it made no difference to me if I died, but that was only in my mind; in my heart, I had been expecting to come back alive all along. At that moment, though, I felt for some reason as if I would never return alive. However, my depression did not last as far as Kanagawa. (XIII, 359)

The elation that he expressed in a letter when he first received permission to leave for the front more truly expressed his mood: "My

happiest moments until today have been when I first knew I could
leave for Tokyo [from Matsuyama in 1883] and when I first heard I
could accompany the army" (XVIII, 526). But his enthusiasm soon
turned to bitterness over the contemptuous way the army treated
journalists, and then to disappointment, when the Treaty of Shimono-
seki, ending the war, was signed on April 17, 1895, before he even
reached China. Landing at Dairen, Shiki joined his friend the artist
Nakamura Fusetsu and with several other friends, they spent a month
sightseeing around Dairen, Luangtao and Port Arthur, without
hearing a single shot fired. It was during this period, too, that Shiki
met the novelist Mori Ōgai (1862–1922), then serving as an army
doctor.[9]

Shiki's living quarters in China were filthy and overcrowded and by
the time he left he was seriously ill. Third class on the return voyage
was so crowded that he did not even have room to spit out the blood
he was constantly coughing up.

When the ship landed at Kobe, Shiki was too weak to walk and
had to be taken by stretcher to Kobe Hospital. Doctors there,
expecting him to die, summoned family and friends, but miraculously,
he survived. By August, he was well enough to return to Matsuyama.
There he stayed with his friend Natsume Sōseki (1867–1916), then
an unknown middle-school teacher yet to publish his first novel.

During Shiki's stay in Matsuyama, a group of young haiku devotees
who had christened themselves the Wind in the Pines Society (*Shōfū
Kai*) adopted him as their mentor and filled Sōseki's house every day.
Eventually, according to his own account, Sōseki was lured down from
the second floor by their enthusiasm and became one of their number.
Shiki introduced them all to the new haiku style he had been
developing since 1892.

The major lesson the members of the Wind in the Pines Society
learned from Shiki was to compose haiku on topics derived from their
own observation of nature. Since they had hitherto been writing, as
was the custom then, only on assigned topics, with no effort to ground
their poems in experience, this involved a basic change in their
approach to haiku. Of this group, Yanagihara Kyokudō became one
of Shiki's foremost disciples, and Sōseki went on to become one of the
greatest of modern Japanese novelists. Shiki, inspired by his success

with the Wind in the Pines Society, wrote a text on haiku for beginners, *Haikai Taiyō* [The Elements of Haiku], published serially in *Nippon* from October through December of 1895.

In October, Shiki returned to Tokyo via Hiroshima, Suma, Osaka, and Nara. While at Suma, he first experienced the pelvic pains that made it difficult to walk. By November, these pains had become chronic and intense. He wrote to a friend, "I am becoming more and more desperate. I have resolved to fight literature to the death" (XVIII, 630). By this martial phrase that self-consciously harked back to his samurai origins, he meant that he had resolved to dedicate his life to literature: the realization that he was incurably afflicted by tuberculosis and would be incapable of any activity more strenuous than reading and writing for the rest of his life, made him focus all his immense hopes and ambitions on literature. Although Shiki's fame today is primarily as a haiku poet, nothing he wrote at this period gives any reason to believe that he thought becoming a haiku poet was the only way to realize his dreams and ambitions for literature. Rather, he saw (as is clear from the following letter to Kyoshi) himself as "a man of letters" (the nearest English equivalent to *bungakusha*), with scholarship and criticism being as important as creative writing and all being expressions of a general approach to literature which he hoped would be perpetuated by his disciples.

Thus, in this period, Shiki spoke of *Classified Collection of Haiku* as the principal work he was engaged in, rather than the many haiku poems he was turning out at the same time. From his late twenties on, his critical works grew fewer in comparison with his poetry and autobiographical prose; but this, on the evidence of his own writings, was because his energies decreased to the point where extended critical writing and study were no longer possible for him, not because he began to reject the role of critic and think of himself as chiefly a poet.

It is because Shiki thought of himself in this way—as much the builder of a literary school, or movement, as an individual haiku poet—that the problem of a successor seemed urgent to him. He could resign himself to an early death; but the fear that his life would end before he had completed his literary work, filled him with desperation.

Takayama Kyoshi was the only one of his disciples whom he deemed capable of fulfilling this role. But Kyoshi felt unable to undertake the self-sacrificing mission that Shiki demanded. According to both men's accounts, Kyoshi, who at the time was only twenty-two, was intent on enjoying life. He could neither understand Shiki's desperation nor empathize with his enormous ambitions; while he felt a debt of gratitude for the literary guidance Shiki had given him, he did not feel adequate to Shiki's demand.

Shiki had first asked Kyoshi to become his literary successor in a letter addressed to him and Kawahigashi Hekigotō (1873–1937), who was also included in the request, the evening before he left Tokyo for China. Later, while convalescing after his return from China, Shiki repeated his request, this time to Kyoshi alone. Kyoshi hesitated to refuse directly because of Shiki's condition, and simply replied, "If I can, I will."

The conflict between the two came to a head in December, when Shiki, upon his return to Tokyo, attempted to hold Kyoshi to what he supposed was a promise. In a letter to Iogi Hyōtei, Shiki described in moving, if melodramatic, terms the terrible disappointment Kyoshi had caused him and his subsequent decision to rely on no one but himself. He wrote,

My efforts from now on will continue for the span of one life—my own. I should say, rather, that they will end after the span of one life—a life I shall be unable to preserve for more than thirty years. It pains me that I have barely begun *Classified Collection of Haiku* and yet my life is destined to be short. My years of thought on literature will go from darkness into darkness, more formless than a babe in the womb. (XVIII, 639)

Then he described the final confrontation between himself and Kyoshi, and its results:

. . . at last we sat down in a tea room and I opened my final move:

"Do you want to pursue scholarship or not?" He tried to evade me, but I kept after him with questions until he said,

"I want to become a writer [*bungakusha*]. But I don't care if I am famous in my own lifetime, much less after my death. I wouldn't mind pursuing scholarship, but I really don't feel compelled."

"I don't see anything wrong with other people pursuing scholarship in order to satisfy their ambitions for fame. But I would rather not stir up such ambitions in myself."

His answer meant, in brief,

"I'd like to be a writer, but not badly enough to study, which I detest more than anything."

I replied, "Then your aims and mine are completely different."

"I am grateful for your kindness," he said, "but I don't have the strength to accept your advice and carry out your suggestions. What am I to do?"

Ah, my life ends here! Kyoshi is not to be my heir. I am not to be his guide as I thought I would be. My literature gasps for breath. The day of my life approaches the night of death. I remember several times before this when Kyoshi, I can see now, must have been trying to abandon me. But I was unable to give him up until today. A parent loves his child and so remonstrates with him. But a child gifted by the gods needs no advice from the ordinary parents of this world. The child is wise, the parent foolish. But I did not know how foolish I could be. With deep seriousness, I said, ". . . Until now I thought I had the right and the duty to remonstrate with you. I hereby renounce both."

I returned in silence, Kyoshi taking another way back. My steps had been slow before; now they became slower. Hands in the sleeves of my kimono, I drifted aimlessly back to Uguisu Lane. A tear came to my eye. Whether Kyoshi succeeds or fails from now on is no concern of mine. Why then did I cry?. . .

My literature will disappear like dew on a blade of grass, never to bear fruit. . . . I don't let even a drop of sake pass my lips. I grudge the merest smile. I was desperate even before this happened. But now that I am alone, my resolve to rely on no one but myself is growing even stronger. Death comes nearer and nearer. My literature has at last reached its climactic phase. (XVIII, 640–42)

In this letter, Shiki used "my literature" as a synonym for "my life." He had accepted the knowledge that he would die young, but he retained his attachment to life in sublimated form, as a wish for the survival of his "literature." With Kyoshi's apparent refusal to become his literary heir, and what he supposed (incorrectly) to be the earlier defections of his two other chief disciples, Shiki turned back to his work with a new passion. It was as though he had resolved to create, as a substitute for his "child" Kyoshi, a literary corpus that would remain after he died. The rupture with Kyoshi proved to be transitory, but Shiki's sense of desperation and tremendous personal stake in his literature only deepened. The end result—an impulse to achieve the total merging of literature and life—pervades the prose and poetry of his last years.

Meanwhile, Shiki's works had brought pleasing effects. Several newspapers and magazines had begun to publish haiku by the members of Shiki's Tokyo haiku group, the Nippon school (so called after the newspaper which published most of their work). Haiku was still not accepted as a part of literature by most literary critics, but the fact that the poems attracted any comment at all was in itself, Shiki felt, a favorable sign.

By the next year, 1896, the Nippon school had achieved recognition as a power in the literary world. The healing of the breach between Kyoshi and Shiki occurred after Shiki devoted most of his critical essay *Meiji Nijūkunen no Haikukai* [The Haiku World of 1896], serialized in *Nippon* from January through March 1897, to an extended analysis, mostly favorable, of poems Kyoshi and Hekigotō had written in 1896. Thanks to the notice, both poets quickly achieved recognition and were invited to attend haiku meetings and publish their haiku. Though they had actually intended to become novelists, their success at this time led them deeper into haiku until it became their profession.

In 1896, Shiki had read for the first time *Shin Hanatsumi* [New Flower Picking, 1797], a diarylike collection of haiku and haiku-prose (*haibun*) that the poet-painter Yosa Buson (1716-1783) had written in memory of his mother, and been greatly impressed with it on two counts. First, the sense it gave of closeness to Buson, because of its lack of revision and spontaneity, helped him to understand Buson better as a poet, he wrote. Second, Buson's improvisation of sequences of haiku all on a single topic appealed to him very much. Both the use of the diary and the creation of the poem sequence influenced Shiki later, but the more immediate effect of reading the work was to plunge him into a study of Buson.

Almost immediately after the last installment of *The Haiku World of 1896* appeared in *Nippon,* the serialization of *Haijin Buson* (The Haiku Poet Buson, April through November 1897) began there. In this work, Shiki delineated his conception of the poet who came to be identified with his school much as Bashō had served as a model for the previous generation of haiku poets.

In 1897, Yanagihara Kyokudō founded *Hototogisu* [Cuckoo], the magazine of the Nippon school, editing it from Matsuyama under Shiki's direction. *Hototogisu* soon became the leading forum for the new haiku. The following year, Kyoshi, on his own request, and with Kyokudō's consent, took over the editorship, and the magazine's operations moved to Tokyo: the first issue of fifteen hundred copies was sold out the day it appeared and a second printing of five hundred copies had to be ordered immediately.

By 1897, Shiki was completely bedridden, and after that his condition steadily deteriorated. The inflamed spinal cord, a symptom of tuberculosis of the spine, sometimes caused him unbearable pelvic pain, and tubercular boils complicated his condition. Pus streamed constantly over his hips and buttocks, and festering sores caused him torment. There was no treatment, for the disease was essentially incurable. All that could be done was to wipe away the pus every day and wrap the affected parts in cotton bandages. He was swaddled in cotton bandages and oiled paper as if in diapers.

From 1897, Shiki had to wait, virtually immobilized and in steadily increasing pain, for death to come. Nevertheless, he retained a mental energy and an ability to inspire others that drew people to his bedside and enabled him to continue his haiku reform, embark on his tanka reform, and begin a new movement in prose. In addition he carried on a personal battle with death whose engagements, as often witty or ironic as they are poignant, were recorded in three sickbed diaries: *Bokujū Itteki* [A Drop of Ink, 1901], *Gyōga Manroku* [Stray Notes While Lying On My Back, 1901–1902], and *Byōshō Rokushaku* [A Sixfoot Sickbed, 1902].[10]

Tanka Reform, Sketch-from-Life Prose, Sickbed Diaries (1898–1902)

Shiki initiated his tanka reform in 1898, when *Utayomi ni Atauru Sho* [Letters to a Tanka Poet] was serialized in *Nippon* from February 12 through March 3. During the period of writing this essay, and for several weeks afterwards, Shiki was so carried away with enthusiasm that he often stayed up until two or three in the morning discussing tanka with friends or writing. Late in March, this paroxysm of activity carried on from his sickbed finally subsided, and Shiki decided he would take a short trip into the country to see the plum blossoms for the first time in four years. He made the trip as planned in a jinrikshaw, but the small of his back was so painful he could not enjoy the blossoms.

In August of the same year, when the offices of *Hototogisu* moved from Matsuyama to Tokyo and Takahama Kyoshi replaced Yanagihara Kyokudō as editor, Shiki decided to turn the magazine into a general literary journal that would publish work in other genres as well as haiku—haiku-style prose (*haibun*), tanka, new-style verse (*shintaishi*), and both literary and art criticism. Shiki himself began publishing in it short essays in a style that came to be known as *shaseibun* ("sketch from life prose") or *shajibun* ("realistic prose"). As *Nippon* had been the stage for Shiki's haiku and tanka reforms, so *Hototogisu* now became the forum for his new movement in prose.

In January 1901, Shiki conceived the idea of writing a diary to be called *A Drop of Ink* and publishing it in *Nippon* as a relief from the tedium of his confinement. Shiki was in the last stage of spinal tuberculosis, then a fatal disease, when he wrote this and the two other diaries of his final years. The pain he endured was similar to that sometimes experienced in terminal cancer, but of longer duration and with only morphine as a painkiller.

In *A Drop of Ink* (entry of April 20, 1901), Shiki described his physical condition:

Every day, needless to say, I run a fever. I can neither stand up nor sit down, and it has recently become difficult to even raise my head slightly. The pain also makes it impossible to turn freely in my bed, so I must lie still. When the pain is very bad, it hurts to turn to the right or the left, and even lying on my back I suffer as if I were in hell. (XI, 167)

In the summer of 1901, after completing *A Drop of Ink*, Shiki's condition again took a turn for the worse. His mother, Yae, and sister Ritsu were unable to leave his side at all, and Itō Sachio (1864–1913), Hekigotō, Kyoshi, Samukawa Sokotsu (1875–1954), and

others of his disciples took turns keeping watch at his bedside and
trying to divert him.

By the fall of 1901, when he began the private diary *Stray Notes
While Lying On My Back*, Shiki was not only a cripple, covered with
boils and pus as described above, but was, according to his own
description, beset by the following symptoms: swollen ankles and legs;
diarrhea; indigestion and flatulence; nosebleeds; eyes so painful he
could not read without sunglasses; such difficulty in concentrating
because of his pain, that he read virtually nothing but newspapers and
magazines; and terrible headaches which, from his descriptions, may
have been migraines or the result of sheer hysteria and frustration.
Sometimes his torment was so great that he was unable to read or
write at all. When he began to write *Stray Notes While Lying On My
Back* and, in the following year, *A Sixfoot Sickbed*, he was only free
from pain when he had just taken morphine; but since the amount he
could take was restricted, the relief never lasted long.

In January 1902, after Shiki had written the first part of *Stray
Notes While Lying On My Back*, Hekigotō and his family moved
into a house near Shiki's. This made life more pleasant for Yae and
Ritsu, for they now had female companions nearby and in addition
Hekigotō often took one or the other of them with his family on trips
to the country. This was one of Shiki's greatest consolations, for, as he
wrote, "Their pleasure is my pleasure" (XII, 550).

By March 1902, Shiki was so weak he had to stop writing; *Stray
Notes While Lying On My Back* broke off, not to be resumed until
June and July 1902, under the title "1902: Morphine Diary," with
most of the entries very brief. Shiki wrote in the diary that he was
taking morphine two to four times a day as well as stomach medicine
and sedatives.

By April and May 1902, his condition was worse. In the essay *Byōshō Kugo* [Words of Pain from a Sickbed], which he had to dictate
because he was too weak to write himself, he said that he could not
move his body, and that only if he took two or three doses of painkiller
a day was he able to achieve for even a while a sense of well-being. He
could not think at all and even reading the newspaper confused him,
nor could he write or even talk with any degree of coherence. In May,

apparently with the help of morphine and other drugs, he was able to resume writing, and commenced the third diary of his final years, *A Sixfoot Sickbed.* In its entry for June 19, 1902, he described himself like this:

Here is a sick man. His body hurts and has so little strength he can barely move. The smallest incident drives him to desperation, his eyes are unable to focus, he cannot read books or newspapers. Still more, he is incapable of taking up a brush to write. And shall he be without a companion by his side, or a visitor with whom to talk? *How shall he pass the days? How shall he pass the days?* [emphasis in original]. (XI, 282)

On September 11, Shiki's feet suddenly swelled up so much that he wrote they looked like little vases stuck onto his match-stick thin legs. Three days later, again in *A Sixfoot Sickbed,* he wrote,

I have legs—legs like one of the Guardian Deva Kings.[11] I have legs—they feel like someone else's. I have legs—like huge immovable stones. If one so much as touches them, heaven and earth quake; and all the earth's plants and trees cry out. (XI, 379)

Hekigotō wrote a moving description of Shiki recording his death-bed haiku four days later, late in the morning of September 18. According to Hekigotō's account, he had been summoned to Shiki's bedside at ten that morning with the news that Shiki was in very poor condition. When he rushed there, Kuga Katsunan's wife (the Kugas were also neighbors) and Shiki's sister Ritsu were sitting by Shiki's bed; his mother had gone to fetch medicine from the doctor, for Shiki's throat was so stuffed with phlegm that he could not cough. When Hekigotō asked Shiki how he was, there was no reply; Shiki just gestured slightly with his left hand a few times. He lay, as usual, on his back. Hekigotō conversed with Mrs. Kuga and Ritsu in low tones. When the subject came up of whether or not they should call Kyoshi, Shiki managed to utter, "Call Kyoshi, too." Hekigotō immediately went to Kuga's home next door, phoned Kyoshi, and told him to come at once. When he returned, Ritsu was preparing some sumi ink by Shiki's bed. Hekigotō's account describes how Ritsu held

Shiki's usual writing board for him, Hekigotō himself placed the
writing brush in his hand, and Shiki, too weak to speak, slowly wrote
out his three deathbed poems, word by word. At approximately one
o'clock in the morning of September 19, Shiki died; he had been
breathing so faintly for some time that it was not possible to be sure of
the exact moment of his passing.[12]

Chapter Two
Haiku: From Infinite
Ambition to the Zero Wish

It is fashionable among Japanese critics today to denigrate Shiki's writings on the haiku as unsystematic, biased, or simply out of date. The first two accusations may be true, but the third is definitely not. Shiki's criticism remains among the most trenchant and enlightening of the modern period.

There is no single work in which Shiki set out all of his major ideas in one handy compendium; but from his writings taken as a whole, a coherent picture does emerge. Three contentions are stressed again and again: first, that the haiku is literature; second, that it must be grounded in reality; and third, that the old-style haiku masters must be replaced if the haiku were to survive.

Shiki maintained three other beliefs which, while not easy to reconcile with the three contentions listed above, were nevertheless important in the development of his thought. These were: first, modern civilization was too vulgar and ugly to provide subjects fit for literature and the arts; second, imagination was as important, or more so, than the faithful depiction of reality; and third, the haiku, with the tanka, was doomed to extinction by the end of the Meiji period. But the three main premises of his thought about the haiku remain the contentions mentioned first above. They were firmly fixed in his mind by 1891, at the latest, although not always made explicit until later.

The earliest appearance of his assertion that haiku deserved to be considered literature was in the essay of 1889 (discussed in Chapter 1), *The Origin and Development of Poetry*. There he had begun by asserting that the haiku, in spite of its brevity, could express deep

31

meaning. This implied that its value as literature was as great as that of such long forms as the novel; since the novel had been unequivocally allowed within the boundary of literature by Shōyō and others, this was an indirect espousal of the haiku's right to the same position.

Shiki began the first installment of *Talks on Haiku from the Otter's Den*, three years later, with a more direct definition of the haiku, in an effort to distinguish it from related but less serious forms of poetry such as the *senryū:* "The haiku," he wrote, "is not . . . a form of humor" (IV, 158). In 1895, in the primer *The Elements of the Haiku*, he finally declared unequivocally: "The haiku is a part of literature" (IV, 342).

Such a statement seems self-evident today; but two facts already discussed in Chapter 1 should be kept in mind: first, the conception of literature, and the sense in which Shiki was using the word here, was one that, only a few decades before, had not existed in Japan; second, most intellectuals had serious doubts as to whether the definition of the word even fitted the haiku (or the tanka). In addition, many haiku masters would have been rather mystified by the assertion, for they still viewed the haiku through extraliterary categories, claiming it was an aid to achieving Shinto morality or Buddhist enlightenment.

The concept of literature was inextricably wedded to realism, for the aim of literature had been defined (by Shōyō) as the depiction of the real feelings of real human beings, with one of the results being an elevation of the spirit, a sort of "noble grace" (*kōshō yūbi*). The second major contribution of Shiki's reform to the haiku—his approach to it in terms of realism—thus followed logically from his espousal of the Western idea of literature. (His writings about realism are covered in the following sections under the development of his style.)

Shiki's attacks on the old-style haiku masters and on some of Bashō's poems again derived from the same effort to force people to see and judge the haiku in purely literary terms. The idea that the haiku must be viewed as a part of literature was not only one of the central ideas of Shiki's haiku reform, but was its necessary and basic premise.

The History of the Haiku According to Shiki

Shiki, looking at the haiku through the eyes of a reformer, naturally saw it as being in a perilous state. His view of the history of the haiku, first outlined in *Talks on Haiku from the Otter's Den* (hereafter referred to as *Talks*), in 1892, was uniformly gloomy. He began by insisting upon the haiku's aristocratic lineage in the court tanka, and its potential as serious literature; however, since reaching its height with the poetry of the great Bashō and his disciples, the haiku had declined and by 1892 was, according to Shiki, in such a state that its survival (and that of the tanka as well) beyond the Meiji period was in grave doubt. The reason was four-fold: first, the lack of compatibility between the basic ideal of all literature and art—noble grace—and the ignoble facts of the modern age; second, the intrinsic limitations of the haiku form itself; third, the incompetence of the old-fashioned haiku masters who held sway over the haiku world; and fourth, the popularization of the haiku since the late Tokugawa period.

Shiki's gloomy prognosis for the haiku's future was but a logical extension of the views most held by intellectuals at the time, for there was a tendency, in the early decades of the Meiji period, to brush aside the haiku (and the tanka) in favor of newer literary forms such as new-style verse and the realistic novel, which it was felt could better express modern ideas. It was only the haiku masters themselves, hopelessly cut off from the new currents of thought, and with an overriding, if understandable, interest in maintaining their own livelihoods, who did not perceive the direness of the haiku's plight. The most they did was make such superficial concessions as introducing new subjects symbolic of Western civilization into their poems. They seemed unaware that a more basic approach was necessary or, if aware, incapable of taking one.

The literary ideal that Shiki propounded as the objective of literature and the arts in *Talks* was "noble grace" (*kōshō yūbi*), a phrase, like "to depict as is" (*ari no mama ni utsusu*) for realism, which he had borrowed from Shōyō. As Shiki conceived "noble grace" in *Talks*, it was associated with the samurai virtues of sincerity and integrity that had been nourished by such military arts as swordsmanship and horsemanship. The implication was that once the haiku had begun to be practiced by the merchant class, its decline had been inevitable.

In Shiki's view, the new world of the Meiji period contained no subjects fit for poetry, no subjects, that is, that could fulfill the ideal of noble grace. In the article of *Talks* called "New Subjects," he wrote:

Some people say, "Men's ideas alter with the times." A comparison of changes in literature with those in politics throughout history makes this obvious. As there are few examples in the past of such enormous transformations as the Meiji Restoration, it follows that ideas about literature will come to differ greatly from what they were. Superficial examination alone shows that today's artifacts are totally unlike those of yesterday. Swords and lances have been cast aside, and cannons echo to the sky. Palanquins are used only as vehicles for invalids, while jinrickshaws, carriages and trains, carrying royalty and commoners alike, overrun the earth. Strange sights like these are everywhere; I haven't time to list them all.

Some people say that if we compose poems on these new subjects, these new ideas, we will never exhaust tanka or haiku. I reply: This seems a reasonable position at first. However, new subjects and new words are not permitted in waka. In haiku, they are not explicitly forbidden; but they are hardly welcomed either. This was a natural development, not merely an outgrowth of the stubborn prejudices of the elders of Tempō: the distinction between the refined [ga] and the vulgar [zoku] applies to everything in the world, whether in nature or human society. (I will not present my views on ga and zoku here; they would not differ greatly from those commonly held.) *And when one turns to the innumerable social matters to which this enlightened age has given rise, or the so-called conveniences of modern civilization, many are the epitome of the mediocre, the quintessence of the vulgar, and totally useless to a writer* [emphasis in original]. For example, what mental reaction does the word "steam engine" evoke? No more than the image of a huge mass of intricate pieces of iron, accompanied by a kind of dizziness in the brain. Or try listening to such words as "election," "competition," "disciplinary punishment," "court" and the like, and see what images they call up—perhaps a meeting between a corrupt politician luring potential voters in soft whispers as gold pieces fall from his sleeves, the voters all the while half-smiling at their own expectations, or else a high-class fellow leading a lovely lady into a chamber with immoral designs. Such emotions, destructive of morals and detrimental to public order leave no room for a single elegant conception or noble thought. Some people contend, "Literature and the arts flourished in the past and are now in decline." It may indeed be so. (IV, 166–67)

In sum, Shiki felt that any attempt to make the haiku relevant to the new age by including new subjects could only result in its further decline. Yet, he also knew, and explicitly pointed out, in another article of *Talks*, that change to accord with the times was necessary for survival and if the haiku made no attempt to reflect the world as it was, it was doomed to sterility.

The position Shiki described was a double-bind. It was not unique to him or to the haiku, however. In the same year that Shiki wrote *Talks,* his close friend, the novelist Natsume Sōseki, clearly summarized the dilemma many Japanese felt at the time: "Unless we totally discard everything old and adopt the new, it will be difficult to attain equality with Western countries. . . . [Yet, to do so would] soon weaken the vital spirit we have inherited from our ancestors [and leave us] cripples."[1]

The second reason Shiki gave for the inevitable disappearance of the haiku was its intrinsic limitations as a form. In one of the most sensational (at the time) articles of *Talks,* he wrote that the mathematical theory of permutations proved that the haiku, because of its brevity, must someday die out—there were only a limited number of combinations that could be made from a finite group of objects, and since the haiku's vocabulary and length were both restricted, it was bound to reach its limit someday:

A certain contemporary scholar conversant with mathematics has said: "It is evident from the theory of permutations that there is a numerical limit to the tanka and haiku of Japan, which are confined to a mere twenty or thirty syllables." In other words, sooner or later, the tanka . . . and the haiku will reach their limit. He says that even now it has reached the point where not a single new poem is possible. Laymen without an understanding of mathematics may find this a very dubious theory. "How can that be? The tanka and the haiku are by nature infinite and inexhaustible. That's obvious simply from the fact that even though millions of them have been written through the ages, all are different."

However, this theory, held by our country's old-fashioned men of letters who are unfamiliar with logic, is mistaken and of little value. The truth is, both the haiku and the tanka are already nearing their end. Just take a look—at first glance, the hundreds and thousands of tanka and haiku that have been composed since antiquity all seem different. But when one examines each in detail and compares them all over a broad range, how many resemble one another! All are artificial creations, the disciple having shed only the master's form while retaining his conception, later generations having merely plagiarized old masters. The only difference between them is that one who turned pebbles into gems has been deemed skillful while he who grabbed maggots from piles of filth has been called a bungler. In fine, not a single new idea has been broached; and, with the passage of time, dull conceptions and mediocre poets have only increased.

Though one may place the blame on people, part of it must certainly be assigned to the intrinsically narrow confines of the tanka and haiku. You may ask, "If that is so, when will the end come for the haiku and tanka?" And I reply: "I can't, of course, predict the time of their total extinction but *speaking approximately, I think the haiku has already played itself out. Even assuming that the end is yet to come, we can confidently expect it to arrive sometime during the Meiji period* [emphasis in original]. The tanka allows more syllables than the haiku and thus, from the mathematical standpoint, the number of tanka possible is far greater than that of haiku. However, only words of the classical language may be used in the tanka and since there are extremely few, the tanka is in fact even more limited than the haiku. I conclude, therefore, that the tanka has been practically played out prior to the Meiji period." (IV, 165–66)

In this passage, Shiki, while frankly admitting that the blame lay with human frailty as well, stressed that no matter how fine the poets, in the end mathematics might defeat them.[2]

Shiki's special wrath, however, was reserved for the old-fashioned haiku masters who set the standards for the contemporary haiku. In the essay *Bashō no Ikkyō* [Bashō's Surprise, 1893], a witty satirical attack on these masters, he described an imaginary confrontation between an outraged Bashō returned from the world of the dead to deal with some haiku masters plotting to enrich themselves by the celebration of the two hundredth anniversary of his death. Bashō angrily confronts them while they are discussing whether a shrine or a stone monument would be more profitable, but they, showing no sense of shame or surprise, happily welcome him to their deliberations. Dumbfounded and appalled, Bashō leaves in silence and the next day inserts an advertisement in *The Next World Times* disassociating himself from any and all haiku masters.

The followers of the haiku masters were, it seems, more naive. In *Bashō Zōdan* [Some Remarks on Bashō, 1893], Shiki described them:

Bashō's haiku have acquired a power virtually identical to that of religion. His many believers do not necessarily follow him because of his character or conduct, nor do they respond to him because they have read his poems; it is his name alone that rouses in them awe and yearning. Even in a casual conversation they do not refer to him by name, but speak of him as "The Venerable One," "Venerable Bashō," or "Sir Bashō," as if he were a great religious teacher or the founder of a religion. In extreme cases, they worship him as a god, and build shrines or erect temples with him as the main image, *viewing him not as a writer at all but as the founder of a religion* [emphasis in original]. (IV, 227)

The picture Shiki drew was an accurate one, by and large. As the composition of haiku had become a popular amusement, lucrative commercial activities had grown up around it. The nadir had perhaps been reached in the late Tokugawa period when a form of gambling called *mikasazuke* arose that was based on the haiku and which became so rampant that it was finally outlawed by the Tokugawa Bakufu. In the early Meiji period, haiku masters still sold their judgments of amateur's poems for a sum, and bought and sold their own professional names as well. For a short time, too, three of the leading masters were even appointed as national officials for moral education, evidence of the degree to which the haiku masters concurred in the didactic view of literature promoted by the early Meiji period government. Shiki's assertion that Bashō was venerated as a saint within the haiku world was also quite literally true. There were religious festivals in his honor, the "Old Pond Church," dedicated to his worship, was at one point recognized by the government, and there were even articles published in haiku magazines (as late as 1881) on such topics as "An Explanation of the Bashō Festival."

In *Talks,* Shiki's attack on the haiku masters relied largely on exposing their superficial knowledge of the haiku and the frivolity of their judgments. One of its articles, for example, was a review of a primer for haiku poets. In it, Shiki criticized the author for using only contemporary poems as examples and insisting on standards of diction that even Bashō could not fulfill. In another article, he deplored the fact that a poem by Hattori Ransetsu (1654–1707), one of Bashō's principal disciples, had been held up as an example of a style unique to Ransetsu, his "ancient tone," in spite of the fact that it was no more than a reworking in haiku form of a poem from the 8th century *Manyōshū*. Yet, wrote Shiki in disgust, so lacking in standards of their own were the haiku masters and their followers, and so eager to follow the newest trends, that even knowledge of the poem's lack of originality would not make them give up their admiration for it providing that they believed that Western scholars of literature praised it for its resemblance to an earlier poem.

At the end of an article in which he showed that a certain haiku's traditional attribution to either Bashō or Bashō's disciple Takarai Kikaku (1661–1707) was incorrect, he wrote:

It is the scholar's responsibility to wipe away such falsehoods and clarify such details. What can one say, then, of the gentlemen-scholars of our time, who seek to mislead novices and rustics by translating parts of Western works and calling themselves the authors, or claiming to be the editors of old works which they have merely reprinted? (IV, 195)

Or, more succinctly, "Since becoming the sport of amateurs and ignoramuses, haiku have become more and more numerous, more and more banal" (IV, 196–97).

The popularization of the haiku and the idealization of Bashō had begun, Shiki wrote, in the Tempō period (1830–1843). In *Some Remarks on Bashō,* he described the process as follows: in the Genroku period (1688–1703), when Bashō was active, the haiku had not been an art for the masses. Many of the haiku of Bashō's disciples Kikaku, Ransetsu and Mukai Kyorai (1651–1704) were beyond the comprehension of ordinary scholars, let alone the uneducated masses. But during the Tempō era, the haiku had become an amusement for the common people. The works of the so-called Three Masters of Tempō (Sōkyū, Baishitsu, and Hōrō) were so simple that, he wrote, "even children and delivery boys can understand them and rickshaw men and stableboys vie in imitating them" (IV, 228). At the same time, Bashō's reputation became so exalted that his haiku were believed to be perfect and he himself was regarded as a god; but people who truly understood his haiku almost disappeared.

Shiki's account of the history of the haiku down to his own time was basically accurate. Its only major distortion was the omission of

Yosano Buson (1716–1783), but this was because Shiki himself did not fully realize Buson's importance until a few years later; the lack was then remedied in his later essays. Shiki's basic point, that by the late Tokugawa period the haiku had degenerated to a popular amusement and was no longer a serious art, would not have been disputed by anyone.[3] What was surprising was his assumption and insistence that haiku had the potential to rise from the status of an amusement and once more become a serious art. This, together with his later re-evaluation of Yosano Buson as a poet on a par with the great Bashō, led to radical revisions in the accepted conception of the haiku and its historical development.

Shiki's views on Bashō and Buson were presented in the essays *Some Remarks on Bashō, Angya Haijin Bashō* [The Voyager-Poet Bashō, 1890], and *The Haiku Poet Buson*. The first work is usually taken as an iconoclastic attack on Bashō because in it Shiki made the statement that nine-tenths of Bashō's poems were doggerel. On the other hand, he is seen, because of his praise for Buson in *The Haiku Poet Buson*, as a slavish admirer of Buson. While it is true that Shiki deserves the credit for the rediscovery of Buson's greatness as a haiku poet, a careful reading of his works on Bashō shows that it is not true that he dismissed Bashō's poetry as worthless.

Shiki valued Bashō as a poet for two reasons: first, because he believed that Bashō had been the first realistic poet in the haiku (see (pp. 44–47) and second, because many of his poems had possessed "sublimity and grandeur" (*yūkon gōsō*). Among the poems Shiki gave to illustrate the latter characteristic were:

> araumi ya   Stormy seas!
> Sado ni yokotau   Stretched across to Sado,
> Ama no Kawa   the Milky Way.
>
> natsugusa ya   The summer grasses—
> tsuwamonodomo ga   Of brave soldiers' dreams
> yume no ato   The aftermath.[4]

The sublime tone was, according to Shiki, unique to Bashō. Although his realism had been successfully imitated by his followers and later poets, no poet after him had achieved the sublime tone:

The most exalted mode in literature and the arts and yet that most lacking in Japanese literature is the essential element of sublimity or grandeur. In waka there were some examples in the *Manyōshū* and earlier, but ever since the *Kokinshū*, with the sole exception of [Minamoto] Sanetomo, this quality has completely disappeared. The poetry of [Kamo no] Mabuchi[5] contains imitations of the Manyō style, but as we approach the modern era, the preference has been for small-scale, detailed works; sublimity seems to have been totally forgotten. . . . *During all this time, Matsuo Bashō alone possessed a sense of grandeur; wielding a sublime brush, he expressed a majestic vision of heaven and earth, and depicted the beauties of nature, to astound an age* [emphasis in original]. (IV, 243)

Shiki found Bashō's work deficient in one area, however: he had not used imagination. In *Some Remarks on Bashō*, he wrote:

Bashō's haiku speak only of what was around him [emphasis in original]. That is, his subject was either an emotion he felt subjectively or else natural scenes and human affairs that he observed objectively. This is of course admirable, but the fact that he discarded scenes which arise from imagination and are outside observation, as well as human affairs he had not experienced, shows that Bashō's realm was rather small.

Four years later, in *The Haiku Poet Buson,* he wrote of Bashō:

He simply took himself as his basic poetic material and went no further than expressing the truth of objects related to him. In modern terms, such poverty of observation is really laughable.[6] (IV, 640–41)

Of all haiku poets, Shiki wrote in the same work, only Buson had used imagination successfully. In this lay his uniqueness, as Bashō's had lain in the tone of sublimity and grandeur, the majestic vision. Using imagination to write haiku, said Shiki, meant writing about what human beings cannot experience, what does not exist in reality, ancient things, places one has never visited, or societies one has never seen. He gave numerous examples of such poems by Buson, many of which require extensive annotation before they are comprehensible. One of the simpler examples was:

> kawataro no   an inn for
> koisuru yado ya   kappa to make love in—
> natsu no tsuki   summer moon (IV, 642)

Kappa are legendary magical beasts that live in rivers and water-ways. The inn might be on the banks of the Yodogawa River in Kyoto near Buson's home. Seeing it in the light of the bright summer moon, the poet imagines that kappa might tryst there.

More typical in the complexity of its allusion was:

> meigetsu ya   harvest moon—
> usagi no wataru a rabbit crossing
> Suwa no umi   Suwa Lake (IV, 642)

In the moonlight, the motion of the wavelets on the lake suggests a white rabbit jumping from one wave to the next. This peculiar conjunction of images was derived from a line in the Nō play *Chikubushima*, "When the moon floats upon the water, it seems as though a rabbit too is running on the waves." The familiar image of the rabbit who beats rice cakes on the moon also comes to mind.

Shiki characterized the beauty associated with Bashō's sublime tone as "simple beauty." It was imprecise in the sense that it gave the broad outlines but not the details. Its lack of precision left room for the overtones that were associated with it. In contrast to this was the precise beauty of later poets, such as Buson, who tended to describe small or medium scale scenes and to examine one thing closely. Where the charm of simple beauty lay in its overtones, that of precise beauty lay in its clarity of impression. Here are a few of Shiki's many examples of Buson's precise beauty:

> uguisu no   the bushwarbler
> naku ya chiisaki sings, its
> kuchi akete   small mouth opening (IV, 647)

> tenteki ni   struck by a
> utarete komoru   raindrop, snail
> katatsuburi   closes up (IV, 647)

> botan chitte   peony petals
> uchikasanarinu   scatter, pile up—
> ni san pen   two, then three (IV, 647)

tsurigane ni	alighted
tomarite nemuru	on a temple-bell,
kochō kana	a napping butterfly (IV, 636)

As simple beauty was characteristic of earlier poetry and precise beauty of later, so negative beauty gave way in the history of literature to positive beauty. Bashō's poems tended toward the former, by which Shiki meant such ideals as classical grace (*koga*), mystery and depth (*yūgen*), pathos (*hisan*), tranquility (*chinsei*), simplicity (*hei-i*), subdued elegance (*sabi*), and thinness (*hosomi*). Buson's, on the other hand, tended toward the positive traits of virility (*yūkon*), strength (*keiken*), charm (*enrei*), and vitality (*kappatsusa*).

In general, Oriental literature and art were characterized by negative beauty while Western literature and art tended toward positive beauty. Yet, within the history of Japanese poetry, as within art and literature as a whole, negative beauty was characteristic of earlier periods and positive beauty of later ones.[7]

Since Shiki's analysis treats the history of the haiku as a kind of evolution, one might expect that in the end he would firmly maintain that Buson was a better poet than Bashō. But in fact he went out of his way to deny this, explicitly stating in *The Haiku Poet Buson* that while Buson and Bashō were opposites in every way, they were the two greatest haiku poets who had ever lived and he did not consider either better than the other.

In reconsidering Shiki's early attack on Bashō in 1893, then, it is well to take his remarks of 1897 in *The Haiku Poet Buson* into account. It is also important to remember that even though he dismissed nine-tenths of Bashō's poems as doggerel in 1893, he went on to add that the remaining tenth were enough to justify his high reputation. Shiki's iconoclastic remarks on Bashō in 1893 must be seen as part of his overall effort to make people apply the standards of literature to the haiku rather than respond unthinkingly on the basis of extraliterary factors such as who the author was or if his poems taught a moral lesson. He may have been extreme in this one essay, but when viewed in the context of the rest of his work, Shiki's reputation as an unrelenting critic of Bashō is seen to be unfounded.

Shiki expressed the belief that the haiku would die out by the end of the Meiji period, yet he ensured its survival into our own. First, he continuously insisted that the haiku was a part of literature and treated it as such in his criticism. For example, his analyses of Bashō and Buson were made from the point of view of literature as a whole, and the concepts he developed through them for analyzing the haiku were applicable to all literature and the arts. This sort of approach helped diminish the power of the old-fashioned haiku masters who had persisted in seeing the haiku as a didactic form and brought about a fundamental change in the common attitude toward the haiku, conferring upon it the intellectual respectability that Shōyō had given to the novel and the drama.

On a more concrete level, Shiki maintained the existence of the haiku by writing haiku himself and encouraging others to do so. His own compositions and those of his followers were published in his haiku column in *Nippon* from 1893 and in *Hototogisu* from 1897. In 1898, *Shin Haiku* [The New Haiku], a collection compiled under his direction, appeared. It contained over five thousand poems by more than six hundred poets, all of which had first appeared in his haiku column in *Nippon*. After the editorial offices of *Hototogisu* moved to Tokyo in 1898, other haiku magazines associated with what came to be called the Nippon school (or the Negishi school) began to appear in Shizuoka, Akita, Osaka and other provincial areas. Then, in addition to Shiki's own critical works, several of his disciples, including Kyoshi, Hekigotō, Naitō Meisetsu (1847-1926), and Satō Kōroku (1874-1949), published works for aspiring poets.

Shiki also changed the accepted view of Japanese poetic history through his haiku criticism. When he began his reform, Buson was disregarded as a poet, known only as a painter. His comparison and contrast of Bashō and Buson were in effect a new diagram of the history of the haiku, one that is still accepted today, insofar as it makes a basic insistence on the greatness of the two poets. Shiki's essay on Buson was followed by several now standard volumes of commentary on his poems by Shiki and his disciples.[8] Today, thanks almost solely to this work, Buson is acknowledged as one of the four greatest haiku poets (the others being Bashō, Kobayashi Issa (1763-1827), and Shiki himself).

Shiki's essays dealing with Buson created a central figure who served as a unifying force for the Nippon group, much as Bashō had

for older groups. The Nippon group came to observe the anniversary
of Buson's death each year just as the old schools had celebrated
Bashō's, although not with the same excesses. Shiki and his disciples
never built temples to Buson or acquired a worshipful attitude to him;
but in other ways Shiki adopted the forms he had scorned in the old
haiku masters. He claimed that he belonged to no line or school of
poets. But in fact he created his own school and the line of poets he
founded still exists today.[9] He himself may have been free of tradition,
but he created it for others—which is, perhaps, the mark of a true
revolutionary.

Evolution of a Haiku Poet: 1892–1902

In at least two essays, Shiki described his becoming a haiku poet as
something that happened so naturally he could hardly set a date to it.
As stringing together seventeen syllables was an amusement almost
anyone indulged in at times, he, too, he wrote, had done so. And he
had even, at age seventeen, as mentioned in Chapter 1, showed ten of
his poems to Ōhara Kijū at the urging of a friend. But he did not
really become carried away by his interest in the haiku until he began
the compilation of *Classified Collection of Haiku* in 1892.

Shiki came to the haiku, then, as an amateur, a nonspecialist. This
fact is important because it means he had no vested interest in
maintaining the prestige or style of any particular school. In his
readings for *Classified Collection of Haiku,* he began with the *renga*
("linked verse"), the predecessor of the haiku, and then worked his
way up historically until he reached the Meiji period. By going back
to the primary sources, he was able to come to his own conclusions
about the nature and history of the haiku, completely bypassing the
secondhand versions of the haiku masters who were the custodians of
its tradition. The conceptions which he thus acquired differed radically
from theirs, as we have seen, and were later expounded in his criticism.

Late in 1891, when Shiki began studying the haiku historically as
preparation for *Classified Collection of Haiku,* his enthusiasm was first
aroused by the poems of Bashō. As he wrote in 1902:

When I first read [Bashō's collection] *Sarumino* [The Monkey's Cloak]
each poem seemed more interesting than the next, and I found myself

enthralled. . . . This was my first step in haiku. Feeling as though my eyes had been opened a little, I could not wait to take a trip, and spent about three days in Musashino, [writing haiku]. (V, 462)

Shiki took Bashō's travel diaries as works of literal truth and the poems in them as faithful descriptions of real scenes which fitted his own ideal of realism.[10] From 1892, when he "made haiku almost my whole life," he set out to imitate Bashō's poem-journeys. In early 1891, he had already made two such journeys, which had resulted in *Kakuremino* [The Cloak of Invisibility] and *Kakehashi no Ki* [Record of the Hanging Bridge]. In 1892, he traveled as far as Oiso and Hakone in order to write haiku on natural scenes.

By the time he returned to Tokyo, he felt he had begun to understand *sabi*, one of Bashō's central aesthetic ideals. By early winter of 1892, when he went to Takao to view the maple leaves, he had at last become able to write about natural scenes with some felicity. Though the poems he composed were about commonplace and insignificant places, he later wrote, it was not until then that he had even realized such scenes could become poems. Before discussing the poems that resulted from these early journeys-in-search-of-poetry, it would be well to give some examples of Shiki's writings about the poem-journey, in order to clarify his idea of realism.

Applying Shōyō's idea of realism to the haiku, Shiki had already concluded that it had to be based upon the realistic observation of nature rather than the puns or fantasies often relied on by the old school. From Bashō, he then acquired the idea that the best way to observe nature was through the poem-journey. He held to this belief as late as 1897, when he wrote in the essay *Haikai Hogukago* [Haiku Wastebasket]:

In depicting real sights, the best way to create a good haiku is to journey in search of naturally beautiful scenes. Bashō, arriving at Cape Izumo in Echigo, gazed out on Sado and wrote:

araumi ya	Stormy seas!
Sado ni yokotau	Stretched across to Sado,
Ama no Kawa	the Milky Way. (IV, 578–79)

In the same work, Shiki also wrote that the beginning poet should constantly take walks and travel all over, in every season. The subjects of his poems need not be restricted to famous places, however; if one looked about calmly and carefully, subjects could be found everywhere. Even in a little garden where one could take no more than ten steps, the poet might find a new subject every day. Thus, it was not the poem-journey itself that was the absolute value, but the observation of nature: the former was the means to the latter.

Shiki made the observation of reality into a strict discipline, the most fundamental exercise in the poet's training. In 1899, he wrote in *Zuimon Zuitō* [Random Questions and Random Answers]:

> You must not stop when you have managed to extract one or two poems from some broad view. Next you must look down at your feet and write about what you see there—the grass, the flowers in bloom. If you write about each, you will have ten or twenty poems without moving from where you are. Take your materials from what is around you—if you see a dandelion, write about that; if it's misty, write about the mist. The materials for poetry are all about you in profusion. (V, 262–63)

Even the clothes one wore when going amidst nature were important. They were to be in the traditional Japanese style—*waraji* (traveler's straw sandals), rather than geta or Western-style shoes, and a kimono; and one should never ride on a train or use a Western umbrella.

In *The Voyager-Poet Bashō*, Shiki summed his view up: "Truly, poem-journeys were Bashō's life and the haiku should be the poem-journey's soul" (IV, 605).

Shiki's prescriptions were based on the assumption that the basic subject matter of the haiku was nature, not the human world (although his later haiku, being equally about himself, fortunately compromise this). As the novelist must acquire experience of human life in order to write a realistic novel, so, obviously, must the haiku poet acquire experience of nature in order to write a realistic haiku. (Indeed, the point would not even be worth mentioning were it not for the fact that by Shiki's time, the leading haiku poets and masters no longer laid much stress on the observation of nature.) Thus, the stress on travel—not so much to see new sights and to acquire new materials, as to practice and make keener the poet's powers of observation.

It is the act of observation, the way in which one pays attention to nature, which is glorified in Shiki's conception of realism. This is well illustrated by his imaginative description of the way in which Bashō composed his famous haiku on the old pond ("the old pond:/a frog jumps in —/the sound of water") in *Some Remarks on Bashō*. In this passage, he discusses the "as is" (*ari no mama*, a phrase borrowed from Shōyō), which was then his term for realism. He identifies it with the style of the best of Bashō's poems, and attributes its creation in the haiku to Bashō, dating it from the composition in 1686 of the old pond poem. His description of Bashō's way of observing nature in this passage views it as an act of meditation, almost religious in nature. He envisioned Bashō alone in his cottage, trying to decide how to change his style. Bored with the current vogue of using many Chinese words, he was not any happier with the styles of the Danrin and Teitoku schools. While brooding over how to originate his own style,

> He felt as though a dense fog had fallen, and simply sat there in a trance, neither asleep nor awake. At the moment when all nature was quiet and all his daydreams had ceased, he heard the sound of a frog jumping into the old pond outside the window. He himself did not murmur them, nor did anyone speak, but the lines, "A frog jumps in: the sound of water" reached his ears. As though awakening from a dream for the first time, he inclined his head for a moment and then raised it, and a broad smile broke out upon his face.

Shiki went on to say that some people believed that the poem recorded a Zen experience of *satori*. This, he felt, was unlikely, but he conceded that the practice of Zen and of the Bashō (or "as is") style had similar features; in both one must rid oneself of delusions, stop worrying about whether one was skilled or not, and empty one's mind. Then one could write a good poem, and this was how the "old pond" poem had been composed. Shiki concluded:

> ... the sparrow's chirp, the crow's caw, the willow's green, the cherry blossom's pink, are the truth of the Zen master and the essence of Bashō's style. *The old pond poem truly "describes as is"—the "as is" became a poem* [emphasis in original]. (IV, 235–36)

Shiki never again so bluntly compared the result of observing nature to *satori*. But later statements indicate that the act of observation was so intense for him that it sometimes became an almost mystical experience. There is no contradiction between Shiki's image of the poet as a meticulous observer of reality in the essays quoted above, and the image of the poet as a second creator in *Haiku Wastebasket*: "The writer takes his raw materials from nature, then refines them and makes them part of his own imagination. In this sense, one may call him a second Creator" (IV, 578).

The link between the two seemingly contradictory ideas is provided by the feeling expressed in two entries from *A Sixfoot Sickbed* that, as he sketched from life, he himself was entering the realm of the Creator:

I had a flowering branch placed by my pillow. As I faithfully sketch it, I feel I am gradually coming to understand the secrets of Creation. (XI, 344)

"One of the joys of sketching from life lies in pondering how to obtain a slightly darker red or a rather more yellowish one. When the gods first dyed the flowers did they too lose themselves in musings like this? (XI, 344)

With the above discussion of Shiki's views on the poem-journey and realism in mind, we can trace the evolution of his style. A comparison of some of the poems he wrote from 1892–1895, the years in which his mature style was developing, with those from the 1880s, when he still knew nothing but the "banal" (*tsukinami*) style of the late Tokugawa period, is illuminating.

One of Shiki's earliest haiku, from 1885, might have been the work of one of the old-style haiku masters he later so despised:

ki o tsumite	the tree cut,
yo no akeyasuki	dawn breaks early
komado kana	at my little window (I, 7)

Because he has cut a branch of the tree outside his window, more light can enter the room; thus the dawn, which comes early in summer anyway (*akeyasuki*, "dawn breaks early," is a season word for summer) seems to come even earlier. This poem requires the reader to supply a logical connection, to think, rather than feel, his or her way into the poem. In other words, the poem's center is an idea, the idea that cutting the tree alters the apparent speed of time. It is a clever observation, but hardly qualifies, by Shiki's later standards, as a poem.

In 1886, Shiki wrote:

> hitoezutsu   scatter layer
> hitoezutsu chire   by layer, eight-layered
> yaezakura   cherry blossoms! (I, 8)

This poem is based on an implied comparison between "eight-layered" cherry blossoms and ordinary "single-layered" ones. Ordinary cherry blossoms scatter while in full bloom, and the sight is tradition-ally considered one of the most beautiful of spring. The poem assumes that "eight-layered" cherry blossoms scatter the same way; hence the poet begs them to scatter layer by layer so that he can prolong the pleasure of watching their fall.

The poem is completely unrealistic, however. First of all, "eight-layered" cherry blossoms, in contrast to ordinary ones, do not scatter while in full bloom, but wither on the branch. Secondly, their name, "eight-layered" is no more than a poetic description; they are not eight-layered but merely have many more petals than ordinary cherry blossoms—it would be impossible for them to fall layer by layer.

Shiki wrote this poem only two years after writing his first haiku and when he still, by his own account, believed that beauty was a sort of pleasure that arose from the exercise of the intellect. Thus the play of words of "layered"/"eight-layered" (*hito-e/ya-e*) is the poem's center, although Shiki later rejected such verbal play with much distaste.

In 1887, the year of the meeting with Ōhara Kijū, Shiki's poetry was much the same:

> meigetsu no   at the full moon's
> deru ya yurameku rising, the silver-plumed
> hanasusuki   reeds tremble (I, 10)

As the full moon rises, the silver-plumed reeds, which have been awaiting it eagerly, tremble with excitement. In later poems, Shiki would avoid the use of personification, particularly of this sentimental sort, for, like word play, it interposed something between the reader and the natural scene.

Another poem from the same year was:

> chiru hana ni   entangled with
> motsururu tori no   the scattering cherry blossoms—
> tsubasa kana   the wings of birds! (I, 9)

The image of the falling blossoms catching in the wings of the birds (or bird) is quite lovely; but the word "entangled" is an exaggeration. Shiki would not allow himself such idealization in later works. One is reminded here of Shiki's surprise when he found he could write poems about the trivial, seemingly insignificant scenes of daily life. Here, clearly, he was still seeking the startling image, the breath-taking, "poetic" scene.

The poems from the winter of 1892 belong to a different world. On first reading they seem less polished than his earlier poems, even somewhat banal. This, however, is only because Shiki had stopped imposing artificial patterns on what he saw before him and was dealing instead with natural scenes as they were, attempting to find the patterns that arose spontaneously from within them. Two examples are:

> mugi maki ya   wheat sowing—
> tabane agetaru   the mulberry trees
> kuwa no eda   lift bunched branches (I, 177)

The poem depicts a sight very common in farming communities. Since mulberry trees and wheat are often grown in the same field, the branches of the mulberry trees are tied up during wheat sowing time in order to keep them from hindering the work of the sowers.

> matsu sugi ya   pine and cypress:
> kareno no naka no   in a withered field,
> Fudōdō   a shrine to Fudō (I, 163)

A shrine to Fudō (one of the incarnations of the Buddha Dainichi, and a protective deity associated with fire) in an unused field would probably be very small, no larger than an oversized doll's house. Its smallness would make a striking contrast to the large, looming pines and cypress standing near the edge of the field. If the wheat sowing poem conveys a sense of human bustle and activity without mentioning any human beings, this poem conveys a sense of winter desolation ("withered field" is the season word) and quietness. As poems, both are clearly superior to the examples given from his work in the 1880s.

Looking back in 1902, Shiki wrote that by 1893 he had come to understand how to write poems depicting real scenes, but had not yet discovered the importance of selection: "I mistakenly thought that any real scene could be made into a poem." Consequently, he went on, he had written too much. In 1893, he produced over four thousand haiku, the most of any year of his life.

From summer through fall of that year, he took a two month poem-journey around northern Honshū from which many haiku resulted. For example, near Fukushima, he wrote thirteen poems on the topic of "coolness," among which were the following:

> suzushisa ya   in the coolness
> kami to hotoke no   gods and Buddhas
> tonaridoshi   dwell as neighbors
>
> mihotoke ni   I turn my back
> shirimuke oreba   on Buddha and face
> tsuki suzushi   the cool moon (V, 464)

Both poems were composed at Manpukuji Temple in Nihonmatsu. The first alludes to the fact that both Shinto and Buddhist deities were worshipped there and the second to the fact that he slept in a room with a Buddhist altar.

The next two poems were written at Fukushima Park:

> mioroseba   looking down I see,
> tsuki ni suzushi ya cool in the moonlight,
> yonsenken   4000 houses

> tsuki suzushi   the moon is cool—
> kawazu no koe no   frogs' croaking
> wakiagaru   wells up (V, 465)

And this poem was composed at Iizuka Hotsprings:

> suzushisa ya   coolness—
> taki hotobashiru   a mountain stream splashes out
> ie no ai   between houses (V, 465)

The poems above are as unassuming and likeable as those on wheat sowing and Fudō's shrine, and, like them, quite apart from the affectation of the earlier poems. Their aim is to describe real scenes, and to evoke such emotions as the sense of relief with which the coolness of a summer night or a mountain stream in mid-day is greeted, and in this they succeed admirably. Yet, there is nothing memorable or compelling about them; they are merely pleasant.

Nevertheless, these poems show that Shiki had discovered a method of approaching reality that guaranteed he would never lack subjects. Once he had discarded the belief that a poem had to be about some famous place, grandiose subject or striking image, observation of the multitudinous natural phenomena around him ensured an inexhaustible supply of subjects. The reason for the massive outpouring of poetry in 1893 was that he was trying out this new method of composition. The more subtle elements would come later.

In the following year, 1894, Shiki began to feel some dissatisfaction with the lack of selection inherent in his approach. He returned to some extent to the conscious shaping that had characterized his earliest poems, although never to their artificiality and affectation. For example, in 1895 he wrote:

> harukaze ni   fanning out its tail
> o o hirogetaru   in the spring breeze,
> kujaku kana   see—a peacock! (II, 186)

This is a completely realistic picture, but has obviously been selected for its beauty. Furthermore, the sounds of the poem reinforce the meaning in a more deliberate way than in any of the previous poems.

The sound of the three "o"s in the second line evokes the gradual opening of the peacock's tail, and suggests through its rhythm, the motion of the tail gently swaying in the breeze as it fans out its full majesty. Then in the last line, the clipped, definite sound of the thrice-repeated consonant "k" closes off the open-ended vowel sound of the "o"s.

The following poem, also from 1895, is today the best known of all Shiki's haiku and can be quoted by virtually any Japanese high-school graduate:

kaki kueba	I bite into a persimmon
kane ga narunari	and a bell resounds—
Hōryūji	Hōryūji (II, 325)

The poem is based on Shiki's experience of hearing a temple bell as he bit into a persimmon (his favorite fruit) at a tea shop in Nara, site of many ancient Buddhist temples. The bell he heard, however, was actually that of the Tōdaiji Temple, not the Hōryūji Temple. The day after his original experience, Shiki visited the Hōryūji and decided that it would be a more fitting locale for his poem than the Tōdaiji, because of its famous persimmon orchards. This, of course, is a very literal example of Shiki's use of selection in combination with realism; but the poem has more subtle elements. Among these, the skillful use of sound is most noticeable.

As in the peacock poem's last line, the use of the repeated "k" sounds in the first line of this poem gives a stiff, clipped rhythm, which here reinforces the idea of biting into something. The stiff, clipped sounds begin to lengthen and spread out with "narunari" in the second line and this process, suggesting the resonant peal of a temple bell, continues with the long, drawn-out double "o" and double "u" of Hoo-ryuu-ji.

The point of the poem is, put most baldly, the juxtaposition of the bite and the bell. This juxtaposition, however, works on many levels: being between the sharpness of the act of biting and the long, mellow peal of the bell, as well as, on a more metaphysical level, the mortal moment of one human being biting into a piece of fruit and the broad, eternal expanse of time symbolized by the bell of the ancient temple.

This haiku may be said to be the first in which Shiki succeeded, through realistic description, in evoking a complexity of meaning that goes beyond literal realism.

The development in Shiki's style in 1895 was not completely spontaneous; the influence of the Western-style painter Nakamura Fusetsu was extremely important as well. Shiki first met Fusetsu through Asai Chū (1856–1907), one of the leading Western-style painters of the Meiji period, and also Fusetsu's teacher at the government-run Kōbu Bijutsu Gakkō (Technical School of Art, established 1876) in Ueno. At the time, Fusetsu was a poor student, with barely enough money to buy his art materials. At their first meeting, Shiki thought that he had a frightening face, and that his clothes were even shabbier than the usual student's. The sketches he brought to the office of Shōnippon were very small, but even so his unusual talent was evident. Shiki was so impressed that henceforth he always used Fusetsu's illustrations in the magazine. Later, when Shiki's haiku group founded Hototogisu, Fusetsu's sketches often adorned the cover.

In 1901, when Fusetsu was about to leave for Europe, Shiki, knowing that he would die before Fusetsu's return, wrote a memorial to their friendship in A Drop of Ink. The following is an excerpt:

The first time I saw him seems almost like a dream. When I think of how much my opinions and tastes developed under his tutelage, and of how his life too, has changed from what it was in those days, I realize that our meeting, which then seemed to me so ordinary, was in fact a great turning point in the lives of us both. (XI, 218)

It was under Fusetsu's influence that Shiki added the term shasei, "the sketch from life," to the two other terms he had used until then to denote realism, ari no mama ni utsusu, "to depict as is," and shajitsu, "reality."[11]

Shiki's lessons from Fusetsu reflected the thinking of Fusetsu's teacher Asai Chu, who in turn had been one of the students of Antonio Fontanesi (1818-1882). Fontanesi, a leading Italian landscape artist of the nineteenth century, had been invited to Japan by the government to teach at the Technical Art School and although there for only two years, influenced a generation of Japanese artists. According to lecture notes taken by his students, Fontanesi summed up his theory of painting in these terms: "The basic method of Western painting is first, correct form, second, balance of color, and third, to always imagine as you paint that you are looking at a beautiful scene through a window."[12] At the same time, however, he prized observation and the sketch from life greatly. Asai Chū told the story of how he and his classmates had been assigned by Fontanesi to make sketches of the Marunouchi district. Dutifully arriving there, they looked all around but could find nothing suitable to sketch, and so returned home. When they confessed their failure in class the next day, Fontanesi scolded them, saying there was nothing wrong with the place but only with them and that if they would only look around them there was enough there to keep them busy drawing for two generations. Such an emphasis on observation cannot help but remind one of Shiki's advice to the young poet in *Random Questions and Random Answers*, "Take your materials from what is around you—if you see a dandelion, write about that; if it's misty, write about the mist. The materials for poetry are all about you in profusion." (See p. 46 for complete quotation.)

Fusetsu's first concrete effect on Shiki was to make him, who had been an unreasoning admirer of Japanese art and had never critically considered its extreme stylization, come to admire the realism of Western art. In the essay *E* [Painting, 1900], Shiki described the many debates he had with Fusetsu and Shimomura Izan (1865–1949), another Western-style artist with whom he was friendly, before reaching this stage. With each debate, wrote Shiki, "I discovered something new." Finally, Shiki was convinced, and, for a time, even reversed himself and rejected Japanese art:

About ten years ago [in 1890] I was a devotee of Japanese painting and an opponent of Western painting. Izan debated their respective merits with me some time around then, but I would not yield. Finally, he explained how the round waves in Japanese paintings differed from waves in the sea; then, drawing a facial profile in the style of Japanese art next to one in the Western style, he pointed out the differences. As might be expected, even a person as stubborn as myself, complete amateur though I was, was half stunned and half struck with wonder by this down-to-earth argument. I was particularly amazed when he told me that in a Japanese-style profile the eyes were drawn as if seen from the front. But I disguised my astonishment by arguing that verisimilitude in form had no relation to the quality of a painting. Afterwards, when I came to associate with Fusetsu at *Shōnippon* and we saw each other almost every day, we began to discuss the same subject whenever we met. Since I was still a passionate advocate of Japanese painting, we disagreed about everything. If I said Mt. Fuji was a good subject for a picture, Fusetsu said it was commonplace. If I said pine trees were nice, he said they were boring. If I said Daruma [an Indian priest and founder of Zen Buddhism in China] was elegant [*ga*], he said he was vulgar [*zoku*]. If I said Japanese armor and helmets were artistic, he said the Western ones were more so. It seemed exceedingly strange to me that two human beings could feel so differently and I thought it over again and again. Then I applied what he had been saying to the haiku and suddenly had a great revelation. If one described Mt. Fuji in a haiku, the poem would easily become banal. Most haiku about pine trees were dull, but those about naked winter trees were often elegant. If one put Daruma or the like into a haiku, it would be overdone. I had known all this before, but had failed to apply it to painting. I realized that just as a person unacquainted with the haiku takes pleasure in reading a poem about Fuji, so we amateurs in art, without knowing why, enjoyed seeing it depicted in paintings, too. Still, my devotion to Japanese art remained unshaken and I was rather offended when they [Fusetsu and Izan] disparaged it and praised Western art. At that point I asked Fusetsu to stop comparing the two and discuss them separately, Japanese art in terms of itself and Western art in terms of itself. In this fashion, I felt I came to understand more as the days passed. After ten months I became rather confident of my views. When I think back objectively on those days, I realize that I had understood for the first time the shortcomings of Japanese art and the strong points of Western art. Finally, I yielded to Izan and Fusetsu. After that, whenever I met someone who disliked Western art, it would annoy me, and I would begin a long argument, concluded in the manner Izan had taught me in the old days: drawing one profile in the Japanese style and another in the Western style, I would declare in triumph—"Take a look—in Japanese art, this is how the eyes are drawn in a profile. Come on now, are your eyes really like that?" Even I was taken aback by my own airs. (XII, 435–36)

In the end, however, Shiki came to accept both Western and Japanese art:

After six months had passed, I came to feel that I knew something about how to look at a picture. By this time I was no longer an unreasoning admirer of Japanese painting, nor did I reject oil painting. Knowing in general what painting and painters were, I realized that until then nine out of ten of my . . . judgments had been wrong. . . . (XI, 219)

Applying the sketch from life to his poetry, during the fall and winter of 1894, Shiki took almost daily walks about his neighborhood in Negishi (he had moved there from Komagome early in the same year) with pencil and notebook in hand, each day composing ten or twenty poems. For the first time, he later wrote, he felt that he really understood the charm and wonder of the sketch from life. Some examples of the poems that resulted are:

ine no hana	rice flowers—
Dōkanyama no	fair weather on
hiyori kana	Dōkanyama (III, 590)

ine karu ya	rice reaping—
yakiba no kemuri	no smoke rising from
tatanu hi ni	the cremation ground today (III, 590)

In 1894, as they worked at the offices of *Shōnippon,* Fusetsu would often make a sketch to illustrate a haiku by Shiki, or Shiki would compose a haiku as a title or description of a sketch by Fusetsu. Some of these works were published in the magazine. Such efforts are evidence that the two were aware of the process of cross-fertilization that was occurring between them and even tried to encourage it.

Fusetsu also made Shiki more aware of the importance of composition and form, a lesson he carried over to the haiku, where it resulted in the greater use of selection already seen in his poems of 1894 and 1895. For example, in the fall of 1894, the two friends attended an exhibit where a pair of screens by the artist Sesshū (1420–1506) were on display. Although they were considered among the artist's lesser works, Fusetsu praised them extravagantly for their excellence of form and composition.

"For the first time," wrote Shiki in *A Drop of Ink,* "I awoke to

form and composition in painting and it made me unbearably happy"
(XI, 220).

In another entry of *A Drop of Ink,* Shiki recorded that Fusetsu had
once told him that if one drew only one or two flowers one had to
make them larger than life; Shiki then added that this comment could
be truly appreciated by a haiku poet.

Shiki had first encountered nineteenth century realism through
Shōyō, in the novel, but this was almost wholly on the level of theory.
He had then discovered in Bashō what he took to be realism in the
haiku. But his own, direct, personal encounter with realism came
through Fusetsu, who acquainted him with the shape realism had
taken in Western art.

Whereas the novel made the human world its primary subject
matter, Fusetsu's art and Shiki's poetry both concentrated on nature.
Indeed, Shiki stated as early as 1890 that he believed the haiku and
the tanka were best suited to nature (this belief, of course, had a long
lineage in Japan as did the link between the haiku and painting). It is
easy, then, to see why realism in art, and particularly the sketch from
life, was what Shiki would try to apply to his own haiku, rather than
the realism of the novelists. In this sense, his friendship with Fusetsu
was not only fortuitous, but pivotal in the development of his style.

From Infinite Ambition to the Zero Wish

Shiki's confrontation with his own mortality after his return from
China in 1895 has already been described in Chapter 1. Here the
long-term effect which his constant awareness of death after 1895 had
on his poetry will be discussed.

From 1896, we begin to find haiku in Shiki's mature style,[13] poems
which touch upon what was to become his most profound theme: his
own suffering mortality juxtaposed to the beauty and continuity of
nature. However, in seeming contradiction, his criticism at this period
was becoming more and more insistent upon the role of imagination in
poetry, even though still averring that it must be grounded in reality.
For example, in *The Haiku Poet Buson,* he wrote:

Just as literature must be based on the actual, so must painting be based on
the sketch from life. But as painting should not be based on that alone, so too

literature should not be based on actuality alone ... [for] the writing of an author of ordinary experience will ultimately be unable to avoid triteness. Literature is not biography or a record of facts. While the author's hand rests upon an old desk in a four and a half mat room, his imagination ranges beyond his country's borders throughout the universe and he seeks beauty in perfect freedom. Though wingless, he can soar to the sky; though finless, he can hide in the oceans. Where there is silence, he hears sounds; where there are no colors, he sees them. In haiku there is only one poet like this: Buson. (IV, 640)

Until the year before he wrote *The Haiku Poet Buson,* Shiki's model, if he may be said to have had one, had been Bashō, and his image of the haiku poet's quintessential activity, the poem-journey. Now his model became Buson, who suggested another possible quintessential activity for the poet, one which, significantly, in light of Shiki's own physical condition, required no movement by the body.

The Haiku Poet Buson was written at a relatively early stage of Shiki's invalidism. Perhaps he had not yet learned to cope with the physical confinement imposed by his illness and felt a need to escape, at least mentally, from its confines. By 1902 when he wrote *A Sixfoot Sickbed,* he had reverted to his original emphasis on the observation of nature. There, in his final statement about realism, he wrote:

The sketch from life is a vital element in both painting and descriptive writing: one might say that without it, the creation of either would be impossible. The sketch from life has been used in Western painting from early times; in olden times it was imperfect, but recently, it has progressed and become more precise. In Japan, however, the sketch from life has always been looked down on, so that the development of painting was hampered, and neither prose, poetry, nor anything else progressed. ... This has become a habit, and even today nine people out of ten still do not appreciate the sketch from life ... and reject it as extremely shallow. The truth is that it is imagination which is shallow and has nowhere near the variety of the sketch from life. I do not say that a work based on the imaginative method is always bad, but it is a fact that many of the works which rely on it are often bad. Imagination is an expression of the human mind, so unless one is a genius it is only natural for mediocrity and unconscious imitation to be unavoidable. ... The sketch from life, in contrast, copies nature, so the themes of prose and poetry based on it can change as nature does. When one looks at a work based on the sketch from life, it may seem a bit shallow; but the more one savors it, the more variety and depth it reveals. The sketch from life has defects of course . . . but not nearly as many as imagination, I feel. With imagination, one often tries to make a flying leap on to the roof and ends by falling into the middle of the pond. The sketch from life may be simple, but it does not result in such failures. And when it comes to possessing good taste amidst simplicity, its wonders truly beggar description.(XI, 289-90)

By the time Shiki made this statement, he seems to have adjusted to the limits of his world. The title of the diary itself, with its implication that his world was contained within the boundaries of a sixfoot sickbed, would indicate as much, as does the title of the diary he had written the previous year, *A Drop of Ink*. Both suggested that he had scaled down his expectations to the point where they no longer created needless frustrations. In 1895, Shiki had written in a letter to Kyoshi:

Many people in this world have great ambitions, but none so great as I. Most people are buried in the earth still embracing their dreams, but no one will ever go beneath the earth holding fast to as many as I. . . . No matter how great my achievement in haiku, it will be as zero compared to the infinity of my dreams. (XIX, 18)

By 1901, when he wrote *A Drop of Ink*, he spoke of his ambitions not in terms of infinity but in terms of nothingness:

In their early stages, human wishes tend to be grandiose and vague, but by and by they become small and well-defined. Four or five years ago, when I first became an invalid, my wishes were already very small. I used to say I wouldn't mind being unable to walk far, if only I could walk in my garden. After a few years, when I could no longer walk, it still seemed that simply being able to stand up would be a joy.

When I told people that, I used to say with a laugh, "How minute a desire!" By the summer before last, I had reached the point where I only grumbled, "I'm not hoping to stand—I only ask the god of sickness to let me sit up." But my wishes had not stopped shrinking even then. Yesterday and today my plaint has been, "Who cares about sitting up? What joy to simply be free of pain, able to lie down in comfort for a single hour!" A miniscule request indeed! My wishes are now so reduced they can shrink no more. The next and final stage will be the zero wish—would Shaka have called it Nirvana, and Jesus, Salvation? (XI, 99)

The most interesting poetry of Shiki's last years is based upon the limited world he describes so vividly in the passage above; ironically, it fulfills the criticism Shiki made of Bashō's poems as being based only on observation of what he himself had seen. Yet he was able to see much less than Bashō because he could not walk or travel. The poetry of Shiki's last years, in brief, is a poetry of poverty. It seems to come out of a world lacking in everything—space, health, time, money, food, even, at times, human companionship.

From 1900, Shiki realistically expected his life to end any day. In the entry of *A Sixfoot Sickbed* for August 20, about a month before his death, he wrote of how he felt at having used up one hundred of the envelopes *Nippon* had had printed for him to mail them his daily entries in:

A Sixfoot Sickbed has reached a centennial. Assuming one entry per day, it has gone past a hundred days; a hundred days is no doubt a very short period, but to me it is as though over ten years have passed. It is an experience unknown to other people, I suppose, but these days when I realize that something I must do will take time, I am bothered from the first by how long it will take. It is hardly worth mentioning, but it was annoying having to write *A Sixfoot Sickbed*, put it in an envelope for mailing to the newspaper and then write the address on it every day, so I asked the paper to have the envelopes printed for me. (XI, 354)

He went on to say that although he had only asked for one hundred, he even then worried that they might laugh at him for thinking he would live that long; nevertheless, they had printed three hundred. Now he was surprised to discover he had actually used up a full one hundred. He concluded,

People won't understand my happiness at having survived this long period of one hundred days. However, two hundred envelopes still remain; two hundred days is over half a year. In over half a year, the plum blossoms will be out. Will they really bloom before this sick man's eyes?

To live on and to support his mother and sister as well, Shiki had his salary from *Nippon,* but that this did not suffice is evident from his repeated mentions of simple articles, such as an inkstone, that friends provided because he could not afford them himself, and by entries like the one in *Stray Notes While Lying On My Back* describing his intense wish to order an expensive meal from a restaurant and the impossibility of doing so unless he sold his books. In the last year or so of his life, he could not even enjoy food, however, because in addition to his earlier inability to digest it well, his teeth and gums were so badly decayed that he could not chew.

The best poems of the last years—mostly from 1900 on, but some from as early as 1896—are like drops squeezed from a nearly dried up brush, to borrow the metaphor implied by the title "a drop of ink." They are strong but sparse, laconic but evocative. It is true of them, as Shiki wrote of the sketch from life in *A Sixfoot Sickbed,* that they may at first seem shallow, but the more one savors them, the more variety and depth they reveal.

Such poems are difficult to appreciate for readers accustomed to thinking of poetry as a lyrical overflowing of emotion. The problem is compounded by the resistance of many of them to translation. Haiku are notoriously difficult to translate in any case, but even among haiku poets, Shiki's later poems in the sketch from life style are surely among the least amenable to translation. They rarely make their point by an image or metaphor that takes the reader at once with its beauty, as, for example, Bashō's often do—to give only one illustration, his (Bashō's):

> takotsubo ya   octopus pots—
> hakanaki yume o   floating dreams beneath
> natsu no tsuki   the summer moon.

Some, in fact, are so simple and bare that in translation they are difficult to differentiate from the most banal prose. Successive readings, however, often reveal a deeper universal meaning beneath the surface one. The poems tend to become more evocative the more they are read—in a word, they grow on one, in a way that more immediately striking poetry does not always do.

The following poem of 1896 illustrates this combination of surface simplicity and deeper complexity:

furuniwa ya	old garden—she empties
tsuki ni tanpo no	a hot-water bottle
yu o kobosu	under the moon (III, 254)

The overt content of this poem is indeed simple: someone (unspecified, but one might imagine Shiki's mother or sister) is pouring out the water from a hot-water bottle into an old garden lit up by the moon. Yet, there is more to it than that. The poem juxtaposes a conventionally beautiful object (the moon) with a banal, everyday one (an invalid's hot-water bottle) against the background of an old garden. The sound pattern of the third line emphasizes the juxtaposition of the moon and the hot-water bottle: the pattern of a two-syllable noun beginning with "t" (*tsuki, tampo*) and followed by a one-syllable preposition beginning with "n" (*ni, no*) is repeated twice. Although the two images are opposite in their associations, their placing within the poem emphasizes their similarity as sounds, so that they become complementary opposites, each highlighting the other: as the moon reveals the hot-water bottle on a literal level (one could not see the bottle without the moon, or at least could not see it as well), so the hot-water bottle, on a figurative level, sets off the beauty of the moon by its own banality.

Additional associations are possible. For example, if one takes *tsuki ni* to mean not only "under the moon" (or more literally, "in the presence of the moon"), but also as meaning "onto the moon" or "into the moon," which are other possible meanings, then the moonlight is being reflected in the water poured from the hot-water bottle and the moon and water are united in a fusion of light and liquidity.

Or, again, one may take the hot-water bottle as shorthand for the invalid who used it, that is, Shiki himself, and pursue yet another train of association: the moon will go on after both the garden and the invalid are gone. Yet here, as the moon and the water from the bottle are, for a moment, one, so too the invalid, by extension, knows a moment of immortality, of respite from his own mortality. This, finally, is the meaning of the poem. The tawdry mortality of the hot-water bottle and of the invalid who depends on it is seen for a moment in the light of immortality and beauty.

Shiki's use of two conventional images, the moon and the old garden, made this poem rather easy to appreciate with a little thought. By 1900, however, his poems were not always as accessible. This, one of his most famous, and controversial, is a prime example:

"teizen"	"Before the Garden"
keitō no	cockscombs . . .
jūshigohon mo	must be 14,
arinubeshi	or 15 (III, 359)

The headnote to the poem indicates that Shiki was on the veranda looking out at the garden. The poem is a comment on the cockscombs—he has tried to count them and that is his estimate.

Cockscombs are a brilliant red autumn flower, about two feet tall, and very straight. Their petals, bunched close together, look like masses of stiff, ruffled velvet, and they grow in clusters that would make it difficult to count their precise number. A group of them gives the impression of a fiery blaze of red.

Shiki wrote the poem at a haiku meeting attended by eighteen of his disciples on September 9, 1900. Only two of those present chose it as the best, which made it the least popular of all the poems submitted at the meeting. Takahama Kyoshi did not even consider the poem worth including in the collection of Shiki's haiku, *Shiki Kushū*, that he compiled shortly after Shiki's death. The poem was first praised by Shiki's tanka disciple Nagatsuka Takashi (1879–1915) and later by the greatest tanka poet of this century, Saitō Mokichi (1882–1953). It remains a controversial poem even today, however, with some critics maintaining that it is no more than a commonplace description in which the details of number and the variety of flower are purely arbitrary, and others asserting that it is extremely moving.

The critic Yamamoto Kenkichi (b. 1907), the poem's most articulate contemporary defender, is struck by the contrast between Shiki, the invalid whose body is wasting away, and the vigor and force of the cockscombs which are such a fiery mass of color. The poet might feel oppressed by the flowers' strength, but instead their life moves him, entering him and invigorating him until he is moved to exclaim quietly, with an artless, childlike enthusiasm, over their numbers.[14] After one reads the essay *Shōen no Ki* [Record of the Little Garden, 1898] and realizes the intimacy Shiki felt for the flowers and the plants in his garden, this interpretation takes on even greater credibility. (A translation of that essay is included in Chapter 5.)

Yamamoto's interpretation implies that there are really two elements or subjects in the poem—the life-symbolizing flowers and the invalid Shiki. If the first element, the flowers, is overtly described, the second element, Shiki himself, is only hinted at, by the headnote "Before the Garden" and then by the verb "there must be," a statement of probability rather than fact which presupposes a person making the estimate.

Earlier I referred to one of the central themes of Shiki's later poetry as being the contrast between his own mortality and the continuity of the natural world around him. The cockscomb poem is an early expression of this theme. Here, nature is still consolation, arousing in him a childlike delight; yet there is a second meaning, that of Shiki's own weakness and mortality.

Another poem in which nature arouses the same simple delight with the same underlying poignance is the famous haiku of 1896 on the snow:

> ikutabi mo   again and again
> yuki no fukasa o   I ask how high
> tazunekeri   the snow is (II, 610)

This poem was actually the second of a sequence of four called *Byō-chū no Yuki* [Snow While Sick] in which the poet moves from joy at the discovery of the snow to irritation at his distance from it. The first poem is an exclamation:

> yuki furu yo   snow's falling!
> shōji no ana o   I see it through a hole
> mite areba   in the shutter . . . (II, 610)

This, too, is a simple expression of a childlike joy. The second poem ("again and again/I ask how high/the snow is") merely records the repeated questioning that the poet's joy leads to. Of all the poems in the sequence, it is the only one in which the poet's emotion is not directly expressed. The poet's repeated questioning could come from eagerness or longing, or both. Having read the first poem in the sequence, the reader's first impression might be that the questioning comes from simple eagerness. But further reflection on the meaning of "again and again," with its implication that the poet, lying in bed and unable to go outdoors, has been thinking about the snow for a long time, suggests a certain longing and sadness. One feels the poignance of the distance between the poem's speaker and the snow, a distance that can be bridged only by the repeated questioning.

The third and fourth poems of the sequence document the poet's reactions to this sense of distance. The third expresses boredom and self-pity, the fourth an explosive impatience:

> yuki no ie ni   all I can think of
> nete iru to omou   is being sick in bed
> bakari ni te   and snowbound . . .
>
> shōji ake yo   open the shutter!
> Ueno no yuki o   I'll just have a look
> hitome min   at Ueno's snow! (II, 610)

The first, second, and fourth poems of the sequence each express a single feeling only. The second, however, implies all the feelings of the other three, its bare objectivity allowing, paradoxically, room for greater complexity. At the same time, it transcends each of those feelings as it observes the relation itself between the poet and the natural beauty he loves so much and wishes so greatly to enter into.

In spite of their sparseness and simplicity, their taciturnity, this poem and the one on the cockscombs still achieve two characteristics of many traditional haiku: ambiguity (multiplicity of meaning) and the juxtaposition of the momentary against the eternal. The first meaning of the cockscomb poem is that there are many flowers; the second meaning is that there is very little of the poet left. One is growing, the other is wasting away. The first meaning of the snow poem is how delighted the poet is at the snow; the second meaning is of the impassable gap between him and the snow, his questioning a poignant effort to overcome it.

In the cockscomb poem, the headnote tells us the poet has been sitting on the veranda before the garden, probably for some time. Our knowledge of Shiki's method of intense observation and of his physical condition also reinforces the impression that the poem represents a single moment existing within a long expanse of time. In the snow poem, the phrase "again and again" tells us that the questioning has been going on for some time and the sequence as a whole increases the impression of a long duration of time. Both poems seem momentary fragments existing within a long, enduring silence.

The final effect of these poems, then, is not so different from traditional haiku. Where they do depart from it is in their tone, which is conversational. The first and last poems of the snow sequence are exclamations which presuppose a listener, and read like excerpts from an actual conversation. (This, by the way, is why the translations hardly sound like poetry: in the Japanese, the poems are conversational remarks put into the framework of the haiku form and using the classical grammar, so that they are clearly poetry as well.) The third poem, with its overtone of self-pity, is a mild complaint that could be muttered either by the poet to himself or to someone else. Likewise, the second poem could be either an observation the poet makes of himself to himself, or else a comment he makes to someone else. Because the first and last poems of the sequence clearly have the character of remarks in a conversation, however, it is tempting and, I think, rewarding as a reading of the poem, to imagine a listener for the second poem, too. The imagined listener must be someone physically very close to Shiki, who can hear a whisper, as the poet observes himself. We, the readers, are this listener, allowed to overhear the poet's private thoughts.

The cockscomb poem is also an observation, though of the flowers rather than of the self; and there, too, such a reading seems fitting. In both poems, the scale of the observation is small and near; in one, Shiki observes what is nearest to him, his own self, and in the other, he observes the flowers in his own garden. It is not just the tone of these poems, but also the small scale of their observations, their seeming banality, that gives them the character of remarks made in a conversation. To appreciate these poems, then, one should imagine oneself having a conversation with Shiki—an informal, yet intimate conversation. These are not poems to be spoken aloud in a declarative tone. They are so unassuming, the tone so mortal, that they seem no more than whispers.

This said, it must at once be insisted that the poems possess enormous strength, and are also much more than fragments of conversation. This strength comes partly from the sense of a long period of time that underlies them, and also from their restraint, their objectivity, their understatement. Shiki allows, even requires, the reader to come very close to him. Yet, at the same time, he retains a distance from himself, a self-consciousness that enables him to rise above the apparently irresolvable contradiction between his own mortality and the ongoing life of nature. The strength of these poems, and of Shiki's voice as a poet, comes from this combination of intimacy and distance, from an intensity strangely at odds with the superficially casual tone of the poems. It is the voice of a man who accepted death but never stopped loving life. It is also a uniquely modern voice, as will be argued in the next section.

The Uniqueness of Shiki's Haiku

The expression or depiction of individual character had not been the objective of Tokugawa period writers. With the Meiji period, suddenly and almost without being consciously articulated, there appeared the unspoken assumption that the individual was important, more important than her or his context or situation. The history of Japanese literature since the Meiji period can be seen from one point of view as an attempt by the individual to break out of the molds cast for her or him.[15] Haiku, of course, lent itself especially badly to the expression of individuality and the articulation of complex emotion. One reason was its brevity; another was the importance in it of the seasons.

In the traditional haiku, each poem must have a season word, of which there is a detailed and lengthy catalogue. Furthermore, only certain events and images are considered appropriate to each season word. For example, the way to write a good poem based on the season word "spring rain" (*harusame*) is to find an image or event that goes well with "spring rain" and evokes the natural phenomenon itself—as does this poem by Shiki himself:

> harusame ya
> kasa sashite miru
> ezōshiya

> spring rain:
> browsing under an umbrella
> at the picture-book store

The quiet feeling of spring rain is splendidly evoked, but the identity of the browser is deliberately left vague in order to better evoke the quality of the rain. This vagueness (which can sometimes result in the fertile ambiguity we have seen in the snow and cockscomb poems) is an intrinsic part of the traditional haiku.

One of Shiki's most important accomplishments in the haiku was to make his own individual situation and emotions an essential part of the poem. In his haiku (and his tanka as well), he is as important as the season. Many of his poems still evoke a season or time, but the natural context is usually there because of Shiki, not vice versa. For example, from 1896:

> e no mi chiru
> konogoro utoshi
> tonari no ko

> the nettle nuts are falling . . .
> the little girls next door
> don't visit me these days (II, 569)

When the nuts of the nettle tree began to fall in autumn, the young daughters of Kuga Katsunan (Shiki's neighbor and the editor of *Nippon*), stopped coming to his house to play. In summer, the heat had sometimes driven them indoors to his home; but now, with the fine fall weather, they spent all their time outdoors, forgetting about him. The poem has a bitter-sweet quality that evokes at once the season and Shiki's emotion, half-rueful because of the absence of his young visitors and the passing of the season, half-glad, because of the lovely weather.

In the same year, Shiki wrote this poem about nasty winter weather:

> shigururu ya   it's drizzling . . .
> konnyaku hiete   devil's tongue, cold on
> heso no ue   my belly button (II, 604)

Outside, a chilly winter drizzle is falling. Inside, Shiki is lying in bed, a block of devil's tongue (*konnyaku*) on his stomach. Devil's tongue is a nearly tasteless, gelatinlike food made from a variety of tuber, and usually shaped in block form. In Shiki's day, it was made quite firm and since it retained heat well was often heated in boiling water and then used as a sort of heating pad. In this poem, a block of devil's tongue which Shiki had been using to warm his chest gradually slipped down to his navel as it cooled. The clammy, slightly chilly dampness of the devil's tongue on his navel, quivering as he breathed, echoes the drizzle outside. One feels very intimately and concretely the melancholy sensation of a certain kind of early winter day; yet at the same time there is a faintly amused detachment about the poem.

In 1902, Shiki wrote:

> hige soru ya   getting a shave!
> Ueno no kane no   on a day when Ueno's bell
> kasumu hi ni   is blurred by haze . . . (III, 442)[16]

Here Shiki being shaved indoors is juxtaposed with a lovely spring day outdoors. To be shaved was a rather special occasion for Shiki, and he only had it done when he was feeling much better than usual. As he leans back and relaxes, the sound of Ueno's bell comes to his ears, slightly muffled by the gentle haze of the warm spring day. Shiki's own feelings of well-being and relaxation seem to blend in with the lazy, muffled sensation of a hazy spring day. (*Kasumu*, "blurred," can refer in Japanese to both aural and visual perception; unfortunately, this double use of the word is not as clear in the English.)

In the three poems above, one feels that Shiki and the evocation of the season are of equal importance. Shiki's own emotion is definitely there, but not so strongly that it defines the entire poem. By the last few years of his life, however, there were also poems in which the whole point is Shiki's response to a natural phenomenon. He never goes so far as, for example, the tanka poet Yosano Akiko (1878–1942), for whom the self often becomes so large and emotion so overpowering that nature becomes unimportant, even an abstraction. Shiki never loses balance—it is rather a matter of degree, a matter of how much of himself is in the poem. In the poems of the last few years more and more of his love and longing for this world he was soon to leave permeate his poems and give them a quiet, restrained, but nevertheless undeniable intensity. One example is this from 1902:

"Gabyō Jūnen"   "Sick in Bed Ten Years"

kubi agete   lifting my head,
oriori miru ya   I look now and then—
niwa no hagi   the garden clover (III, 469)

This poem is, of course, about Shiki's garden. Bush clover (*hagi*) is a small shrub which reaches a height of about six feet and puts forth small reddish-purple blooms in the fall. One feels the quiet joy with which the sight of the clover's bright color fills Shiki. As in "again and again/I ask how high/the snow is," a repetitive action on the part of the speaker serves to focus attention on both the natural phenomenon that is the poem's subject and also on the speaker's excitement about that subject.

In this poem, Shiki describes himself completely without sentimentality, and as though he were a third person. His point of view is that of the omniscient author, but an omniscient author with a silent empathy for his principal character. This tone, this combination of objectivity and emotion, is unique to Shiki. It presupposes a kind of self-consciousness or awareness of the self that does not seem to have existed in Japanese writers prior to the Meiji period, no matter how freely they expressed their emotions (and many did). At the same time, this tone assumes an intimacy with the reader. It is private; we are invited, if only very obliquely, into the poet's mind.

Other, earlier poets seem to be talking to us directly, as when Kakinomoto Hitomaro (fl. ca. 680–700) in his *chōka* on parting from his wife (*Manyōshū* II, 135–137) tells us that he thought he was a brave man but now his sleeves are wet with tears. Still others, like

Bashō, speak of their inner thoughts, but in a tone far more exalted than Shiki's. Bashō's deathbed haiku was:

> tabi ni yande   ill on a journey,
> yume wa kareno o   my dreams wander
> kakemeguru   over withered moors

Bashō's tone is a public one. The poem is a good example of what Shiki called Bashō's "tone of grandeur." To mention his illness and in the same breath to draw an image of overcoming it in dream—there is a grandeur and nobility to the poem, the grandeur and nobility of the artist proclaiming or still believing that in the end imagination is stronger than mortality. This tone is totally lacking in Shiki, who would never have made any such assertion.

Shiki's beauty was, in his own words again, "the beauty of precision." Shiki worked with the small, the finite, the close to home. His tone is completely private. Where Bashō speaks as the artist, and the vastness of his image makes one imagine the entire universe, Shiki speaks as a sick man; his tone of voice seems soft, almost a whisper, and he could only be speaking to himself or, at the most, a few friends. One must, as I have said, imagine oneself physically very close to him to appreciate many of his poems. In

> yomei   how much longer
> ikubaku ka aru   is my life?
> yo mijikashi   a brief night . . . (III, 38)

there is hardly a concrete image. The last line, which is the season word, is also a time word; the rest of the poem is a question about time. One has to construct an image in one's mind of Shiki, lying in bed at dawn, commenting on the brevity of a summer night—the heat, his own discomfort, his despair over his pain, his ambivalence about living and dying.

One may imagine that Shiki's pain, which never ceased for long, had awakened him on a hot summer dawn. While he slept, he had been able, briefly, to forget it and the early death he foresaw; now, reminded of both, he wondered how much longer he would live. Yet he gives no direct reply to his own question, only an oblique comment on the brevity of the summer nights.

The night was short because of the season, but what Shiki must really have felt as short was his own life. Hence, there is an oblique comparison between the night and Shiki's life. At the same time, his pain sometimes made him (we know this from his diaries *Stray Notes While Lying On My Back* and *A Drop of Ink*) desire a quick death as relief from suffering. The poem expresses, using the barest understatement, the tormented wish to die quickly, regret at the ebbing of life, and the wish for his life to continue, all at once. At the same time, beneath the specific question concerning his own life, there is a universal question—how long is life itself?

If there is a continuum from the private to the public along which one may progress by gradually adding more and more "clothing" to one's naked emotions, then Shiki sought to catch himself much earlier along on that continuum than had earlier poets. That is why he tried to dispense with metaphor, simile, and other literary tropes. He wished to depict himself emotionally naked, yet he did so with a restraint and an objectivity that saves his work from vulgarity. Still, for some, the lack of esthetic distance between poet and audience in Shiki's work may make it distasteful, or too demanding. Others can accept both the close-up view of Shiki's poems and the majestic vision of Bashō's. In any case, it is certain that through his unique combination of intimacy and objectivity, artlessness and intensity, Shiki imbued the haiku with a new psychological complexity, and made it a poetic form that would survive into the modern period.

Chapter Three

Tanka: The Consecration of the Everyday

Preparing for Tanka Reform: 1893–1898

Shiki did not initiate his tanka reform until 1898 and his knowledge of the tanka remained quite limited as late as 1895. His earliest tanka dates from 1883, but for at least another decade he followed the conservative *Kokinshū* style against which he later rebelled. Nevertheless, the assumption that a reform of the tanka was necessary underlay all his poetic criticism from the first, and he had a clear idea of the direction that reform should take as early as 1893.

In the essay *Bunkai Yatsu Atari* [Indiscriminate Attacks on the Literary World, 1893], he presented in embryo form two of the central ideas of his tanka reform, ideas reminiscent of those presented in his haiku criticism: first, that the tanka must end its artistic isolation and seek to fulfill the more universal standards of literature; and second, that it must broaden its range of subject and vocabulary if it were to survive. In the section of this essay called "Tanka" (*Waka* in the original), Shiki wrote: "Is the tanka itself banal? Then how explain the many great poems of the past? Or, are the poets themselves insipid? I believe the answer lies there." In response to his own rhetorical question as to the kind of people who wrote contemporary tanka, he gave this list.

— Scholars of Japanese literature
— Shinto priests
— Court nobles
— Ladies of leisure
— Girl students
— Clever men with a bit of learning
— Gentlemen newly promoted to high rank or position
— Young men who want to see their tanka printed in books
  and magazines (XIV, 23–24)

Such people, he continued, wrote either as an act of self-indulgence or else to make money; unless the tanka was taken out of their hands, any hopes for its revival were in vain. He concluded,

In short, there is only one way to restore the value of the tanka today: take it out of the hands of the so-called tanka poets (that is, grumpy old scholars of Japanese literature and worldly men of ambition) and put it in those of true poets. (XIV, 25)

The word Shiki used for "poets" in the phrase "true poets" was *shijin*. This word itself was not new, but his use of it was: prior to the Meiji period, *shijin* had designated only poets who wrote in classical Chinese. In the early Meiji period, the term came to embrace as well poets who wrote new-style verse (*shintaishi*); but here Shiki was using it in still another sense. His usage corresponded exactly to the English meaning of the word "poet," for he meant anyone who composed any variety of poetry, as opposed to writers of prose. His use of the word was predicated on the new conception of literature as a unity possessing common standards, discussed in Chapter 1. In demanding that the tanka be turned over to "true poets," Shiki was asking that it be submitted to the universal standards of literature, as he had already demanded in the case of the haiku. He made this point even more explicitly in 1896, in the essay *Bungaku* [Literature]:

How can people say that for the would-be writer of the tanka the study of the haiku is actually a hindrance? This prejudice comes from the mistaken idea that the haiku is vulgar and the tanka refined. They differ in form, it is true, but in content they have much in common: that is how I would answer the old tanka poets. To new ones, I would say: anyone who wants to write tanka must study the haiku thoroughly, and should regard it as only natural for a writer [*bungakusha*] to work in both genres, the tanka and the haiku. (Many Europeans write not only poetry, but drama and novels as well.) . . . Those who wrote tanka until now were merely tanka poets [*kajin*], not poets unqualifiedly [*shijin*]. To become a poet it is not enough to read the *Kojiki*[1] and the *Hachidaishū*.[2] Even though expectations cannot be too high, the tanka poet should be able to interpret haiku at least a little bit. (XIV, 178–79)

In the same section of *Indiscriminate Attacks on the Literary World* discussed above, Shiki also approached the problem of the limited vocabulary and long tradition of the tanka, which made originality extremely difficult. The only remedies, he said, were to use new words or to write *chōka* as well as tanka. This concern ultimately led him to develop the idea of harmonizing the haiku and the tanka. In the essay *Bungaku Mangen* [Scattered Remarks on Literature, 1894], he argued that of all literary forms, the tanka and the haiku were the most alike; one might even go so far as to say they differed only in length. It might be objected that they also differed in vocabulary and grammar, but these were arbitrary differences, not intrinsic, as was their length. In spite of their basic similarity, however, the practitioners of each had nothing but contempt for each other. If these two literary forms, Japan's unique contributions to literature, were to be improved, the situation had to be changed. "Harmony between the haiku and the tanka" was Shiki's solution.

The first step toward achieving this end would be to combine the content (conceptions, themes, subjects) of the haiku with the diction (vocabulary and grammar) of the tanka. He said, however, that by the former he did not mean vulgar content (*zokujō*) alone and by the latter he did not mean only elegant words (*gagon*) and classical grammar. He did not specify his meaning any more precisely except to say, in conclusion, that he urged the creation of an exalted (*kōshō*) haiku of thirty-one syllables: on this point alone, his intent was unequivocal. Examples of poems that might fulfill his criteria came later, in *Hyakuchū Jisshu* [Ten Poems in a Hundred, 1898].

The phrase "exalted haiku" was deliberately provocative. It must have seemed a contradiction in terms to many of Shiki's readers. The haiku, having degenerated to the level of a pastime in the late Tokugawa period (see Chapter 2), had entered the Meiji Period bearing an unsavory reputation which it did not begin to shake off until Shiki's haiku reform. The tanka, by contrast, no matter how stagnant it became, never entirely lost its aura of elegance, perhaps because of its long-standing relationship with the imperial court. This is one reason why Shiki's attacks on contemporary tanka poets and on the imperial anthologies (for example, the *Kokinshū* and the *Shinkokinshū*) encountered so much more opposition than had his attacks on the contemporary haiku.

The three principles discussed above—that the tanka must become a part of literature, that its range must be broadened, and that the haiku and the tanka must be harmonized—were combined with realism to become the bases of Shiki's tanka reform. Yet although he evolved these ideas between 1893 and 1896, Shiki did not attempt a reform of the tanka until 1898.

A movement to reform the tanka had begun as early as 1893 (the year after Shiki began his reform of the haiku), with the founding of the Asaka Society by Ochiai Naobumi (1861–1903). The Society's most famous product was Yosano Tekkan (1873–1935), who with his wife, Yosano Akiko (1878–1942) and the members of his *Shinshisha* [New Poetry Society], and their magazine *Myōjō* [Morning Star] succeeded in restoring the tanka's interest and prestige as a literary form. Shiki and Tekkan were good friends, although their ideas on poetry were later quite different, and as early as 1893, during a vacation they spent together at Matsushima, Tekkan had told Shiki of his plans for reforming the tanka. Shiki when asked his opinions at that time replied that he had not yet studied the tanka enough to have any. In 1896, Tekkan's first collection of tanka, *Tōzai Nanboku* [The Four Directions] appeared. In the introduction Shiki was asked to contribute for it, he wrote that he would have liked to have been the first to reform the tanka, but Tekkan had anticipated him.

What, then, kept Shiki from embarking upon his tanka reform in earnest prior to 1898? The obvious reasons were his preoccupation at the time with haiku, and his illness, the steady worsening of which limited his activities. The greatest obstacle, however, was the opposition he knew he would encounter from his seniors at *Nippon*, several of whom were serious tanka poets. Their reverence for the eighth century *Manyōshū* and their insistence on the importance of direct experience set them somewhat apart from the orthodox poets of the Palace School (*Outadokoro*), the official descendants of the great families under whose aegis the imperial anthologies of tanka had been made. Nevertheless, they were in accord with the Palace School in their veneration for the *Kokinshū* and the other imperial collections. Shiki knew that if he revealed his own ideas for tanka reform, which began by a condemnation of the imperial anthologies, he would incur their wrath.

Shiki had wanted to publish a full-length essay on the tanka for

several years before *Letters to a Tanka Poet*, his first major critical
work on tanka; but he had refrained, aware of the controversy that
would ensue. He did not venture beyond the brief comments already
discussed in *Talks on Haiku from the Otter's Den*, *Indiscriminate
Attacks on Literature*, *Scattered Remarks on Literature*, and *Literature*. After a group of Palace Poets published their poems and criticism
in *Nippon*, however, he could no longer restrain himself. He asked
Kuga Katsunan, the editor of *Nippon*, for permission to write a full-
length essay and publish his own tanka as well, and so "finally fulfilled
my long-cherished desire." Then, "the grievances that had been
accumulating inside me for years exploded all at once" (XIX, 258) in
Letters to a Tanka Poet.

During the time Shiki was publishing the successive installments of
Letters to a Tanka Poet and for several weeks afterwards as well, he
was, as he had predicted, under constant attack. His respected elder
friend, the priest Amata Guan (1854–1904), rebuked him for his
advocacy of colloquial language, his criticism of the *Kokinshū*, and his
open dislike of such traditional images as the scent of plum blossoms.
Amata declared that Shiki had strayed beyond his province and that
only professional tanka poets had any business expressing themselves
on such matters. Other readers of *Letters to a Tanka Poet* accused
Shiki of trying to destroy the national poetry of Japan (*kokka*, another
name for the tanka), by his advocacy of the incorporation of foreign
words and foreign literary thought. Even Kuga was uncomfortable
and repeatedly admonished Shiki while the essay was appearing. He
also criticized the group of tanka Shiki published in *Nippon* immediately after the essay had appeared, *Ten Poems in a Hundred*; his
criticisms were so extensive that Shiki felt obliged to reply to them in
two letters. On March 19, Shiki wrote to his friend Ochiai Naobumi
that his poems were being "attacked from all sides" (XIX, 258) To
Natsume Sōseki he wrote, on March 28:

I have enemies in tanka both "inside" and "out".... By "inner enemies"
I mean my seniors on the newspaper and other older men with whom I have
social contacts, all of whom remonstrate with me. It would be completely
improper for me to argue with such people, and yet I cannot take back what
I have already said. I don't know what to do. However, having often

experienced failure in tanka, this time I published my articles only after having first obtained permission, and I will not retreat until I die. (XIX, 265)

In spite of the antipathy the work evoked in older and more conservative poets, however, the reaction of younger poets was mostly indifference. For example, Katori Hozuma (1874–1954), who eventually became one of Shiki's leading tanka disciples, later wrote that, while he had been a great admirer of Shiki as haiku critic and poet, he did not at first feel any great interest in *Letters to a Tanka Poet*. The reason for such disinterest was undoubtedly the fact that when Shiki wrote *Letters to a Tanka Poet*, the real center of the tanka world was not the Palace School poets who bore the brunt of his attack but rather the *Morning Star* poets, who hardly figure in the work at all. In this context, his stress on the *Manyōshū* may even have seemed anachronistic. In fact, according to the poet Kubota Utsubo (1877–1967), few of the aspiring poets of the time thought the *Kokinshū* was interesting anyway; they hardly needed its demerits pointed out by Shiki.

The indifference of the younger poets and the opposition of the older poets made Shiki's reform in the tanka get off to a slow start. The following year (1899), however, Hozuma and three of his friends wrote some tanka and they decided to appeal to Shiki to judge them. When he and Oka Fumoto (1871–1951), one of the friends, visited Shiki at his Negishi home, they found his criticism so stimulating that they began calling on him regularly. Within a few months, tanka meetings were being held at Shiki's home with others, including disciples of Shiki in the haiku such as Iogi Hyōtei and Takahama Kyoshi, in attendance. The Negishi Tanka Society (*Negishi Tanka Kai*) was established in the spring of 1899. With about seven or eight poets attending each meeting, the gatherings often went on from one in the afternoon until midnight, Shiki composing and discussing with an energy that made one forget he was an invalid. He was so enthusiastic that his interest in the Hototogisu Haiku Society meetings waned somewhat and if a haiku meeting ended early enough, he would make the haiku poets who could also write tanka stay on, turning it into a tanka session.

1900 was the most active year of the Negishi Tanka Society. At the end of 1899, Shiki had solicited poems for the New Year through the pages of *Nippon* and their publication in the New Year issue of 1900 vastly increased the number of poets participating in Negishi Tanka Society activities. Then, in the same year, Itō Sachio (1864–1913) joined the society. He became one of its most important members and his activities after Shiki died were extremely influential in creating for Shiki's descendants in the tanka the central position they hold today. Soon after this, however, the progress of Shiki's illness made meetings irregular and the society eventually petered out, to be revived only after Shiki's death. Then, under the leadership of Sachio and later Sachio's disciple Saitō Mokichi (1882–1953), the line of poets descended from Shiki, known as Araragi (after their magazine), eclipsed the group centered around *Morning Star*. Until the postwar period, Araragi was the dominant group in tanka. Even today, it claims more members (about 2,000 in 1973) than any other.

Evolution of a Tanka Poet: 1885–1902

Shiki's early tanka were conventional and dull. Two examples, both from 1885, should suffice:

miwataseba	when I gaze upon
yomo no keshiki mo	Yoshino Mountain
Yoshino yama	loveliness is everywhere
ima wa sakura no	now that its cherry blossoms
sakari naruran	are at their peak[3]

The subject, the cherry blossoms at Yoshino, was a timeworn cliché, and the use of the pivot word *"yoshino,"* in the third line (its first two syllables, *"yoshi,"* mean "lovely" and connect to the first two lines of the poem, while its whole *"yoshino,"* is the mountain's name and connects to the poem's last two lines) had been used on innumerable occasions by earlier poets.

arashi fuku	from among
onoe no matsu no	storm-tossed pine trees
ko no ma yori	on the mountain ridge
idekuru tsuki no	emerges the light
kage no sayakesa	of the clear moon

This poem, too, deals with a wholly conventional subject, the moon's rising from amidst pine trees; like the first, it bears no mark of originality in either conception or treatment.

By 1898, however, when he began his tanka reform, Shiki had arrived at some original ideas and begun to put them into practice. The number of his tanka suddenly increased, as though his criticism and discussions stimulated his creativity. This momentum continued through 1899 and 1900, reflecting the development of the Negishi Tanka Society. The poems of these years can best be understood within the context of the ideas expressed in *Letters to a Tanka Poet*.

Letters to a Tanka Poet was a fiercely polemical work, full of Shiki's characteristic mordant wit. The opening sentences illustrated both aspects: "As you say, the tanka these days is ailing. To speak bluntly, it has been ailing since the *Manyōshū* and Sanetomo" (VII, 20). The second letter began: "Tsurayuki[4] was a bad poet and the *Kokinshū* a worthless anthology" (VII, 23). By comparison with the *Kokinshū*, he went on, the *Shinkokinshū* seemed rather good: "It has more good poems than the *Kokinshū*; but one can count them on one's fingers" (VII, 24).

From the thirteenth century on, the *Manyōshū*, with its great variety of themes and styles, came to stand for a freedom and directness of expression opposed to the mainstream of the tanka, the courtly style of the imperial anthologies. Unorthodox poets used the *Manyōshū* as justification for rebellion against the conventions of the courtly style, appealing to the "Manyō spirit" as their ideal. The Shōgun Minamoto Sanetomo (1192–1219), in the early thirteenth century, had been the first of the "back to the *Manyōshū*" poets; the next wave was led by the scholar of National Learning, Kamo no Mabuchi (1697–1769), in the mid-eighteenth century, and the third by Shiki. With the opening statements of *Letters to A Tanka Poet*, Shiki was deliberately placing himself in the rebel, "Manyō" line and outside the classical tradition of the tanka. Much has been made of this rejection, and it was indeed important. Laying too much stress on this aspect of the essay, however, obscures Shiki's basic ideas, which were positive.

Shiki's primary concern was not to tear down the old poetry, but to create a new poetry vital enough to survive the Meiji period. We know from *Talks on Haiku from the Otter's Den* that he feared the

tanka and the haiku might literally become extinct. He believed that
the tanka could not even survive unless it enlarged its limited
vocabulary, tone, and range of subjects, and unless tanka poets began
to judge themselves by the standards of literature as a whole. In
Letters to a Tanka Poet, he wrote that since the vocabulary of the
classical tanka was restricted to words that had been used in the 10th
century *Kokinshū,* and no words of Chinese or other foreign origin
were permitted, the subjects were naturally severely restricted as well.
Furthermore, the tone of the tanka was supposed always to be gentle
and flowing; a forceful or even slightly humorous tone was looked at
askance.

Shiki's remarks in *Letters to a Tanka Poet* and the style of *Ten
Poems in a Hundred* stemmed from two basic critical concerns, which
never changed from 1898 until his death four years later: the wish to
bring the tanka within the perimeters of literature, as those were newly
conceived in the Meiji period, and the need to enrich the tanka (in
tone, subject and vocabulary) with elements from other genres and
other cultures, in order to prevent its extinction.

In *Letters to a Tanka Poet* #3, Shiki discussed the use of strong
tone as one way to enrich the tanka. Tanka poets proudly boasted that
the tanka, unlike the haiku, had tone, or melody (*shirabe*), he said;
but this was because they misunderstood the nature of tone, supposing
that the gentle, flowing one of the traditional tanka was the only one
possible. In fact, there were many possible tones, and poets should use
those appropriate to their subjects and themes.

Shiki was particularly interested in the possibilities of strong,
forceful tone. (In this, he resembled Tekkan, whose *Bokoku no In:
Gendai no Hijōbuteki Waka o Nonoshiru* [Music which will Ruin the
Nation: Rebuking the Unmanly Tanka of Our Time, 1894] also
attacked contemporary tanka for its lack of strong tone.) Shiki revered
Minamoto Sanetomo for having achieved this tone in his poems,
writing, for example, that the tone of the following poem by Sanetomo
was so powerful the reader could actually hear the sound of hail:

mononofu no	Hail strikes
yanami tsukurou	the warrior's wrist guard
kote no ue ni	as he straightens his arrows
arare tabashiru	on the bamboo field of Nasu. (VII, 28)
Nasu no shinohara	

In his essay *Tsuyoki Wabun* [Strong Japanese Prose], written the following year (1899), Shiki wrote that people associated the tanka with the gentle, soft style of the *Kokinshū* and later collections, rather than with the strong style of the *Nihon Shoki,* the *Kojiki,* and the *Manyōshū.* Many, he continued, seemed to think there was something imperfect about the tightly constructed style of Sanetomo or Munetake,[5] but he preferred it.

Shiki's conception of a strong, tightly constructed style was clarified in *Letters to a Tanka Poet* #8. There he praised the poem by Sanetomo quoted above because, unlike most poems, which were carried along by auxiliary verbs like *-keri* and *-ran* or particles like *kana,* and had few nouns, Sanetomo's had many nouns, only a few connecting particles, and two verbs, both in their simplest form. A poem as lacking in superfluities as this, wrote Shiki, was very rare.

Many of Shiki's own tanka in *Ten Poems in a Hundred* revealed his efforts to achieve the elevated, "masculine" tone he admired in Sanetomo. One poem even described Shiki trying to read Sanetomo's poems aloud, and being so struck by their strength that he could not go on:

> kokoromi ni   I tried to speak your poems
> kimi no miuta o   but I could not!
> ginzureba   The weeping of the gods
> taezu ya oni no   fell upon my ears. (VI, 124)
> naku koe kikoyu

The use of words such as *kokoromi ni, ginzureba,* and *taezu,* usually used only in Sino-Japanese writings and frowned upon in the tanka since the *Kokinshū,* as well as the content of the poem itself, created an emphatic tone not found in more traditionally lyric tanka, such as Fujiwara Teika's (1162–1241) beautiful

> haru no yo no   The bridge of dreams
> yume no ukihashi   floating on the brief spring night
> todae shite   breaks off.
> mine ni wakaruru   Parting from the peak,
> yokogumo no sora   a drifting cloud . . .

Borrowing from other genres was another means of enriching the tanka. In *Literature,* Shiki had made it clear that he believed it essential for tanka poets to study other genres. He opened *Letters to a Tanka Poet* #3 with a fierce attack on contemporary tanka poets for their smug self-satisfaction:

Tanka poets are unique in their stupidity and smugness; they are always boasting of the incomparable qualities of the tanka but they can permit themselves this delusion only because they know nothing else besides the tanka. . . . They do not even understand the haiku, the form of poetry closest to the tanka, and suppose that the haiku and the *senryū* [a humorous form of the haiku] must be the same since both are seventeen syllables long. Of course they have never studied Chinese poetry and they do not even know whether or not poetry exists in the West—illiterates of shallow learning! If they were told that novels and the drama, no less than the tanka, formed part of literature, they would gape in disbelief. (VII, 26)

In *Ten Poems in a Hundred*, Shiki actively introduced various elements of the haiku and of Chinese poetry into the tanka. For example:

tobari tarete	curtains drawn,
kimi imada samezu	the emperor's love
kurenai no	still lies abed—
botan no hana ni	on crimson peonies,
asahi sasu nari	the morning sun shines (VI, 116)

This poem has a voluptuosity, in both sound and image, that is closer to Chinese poetry than to the traditional tanka. The scene itself is familiar from many Chinese poems, perhaps the most famous example being *The Song of Everlasting Sorrow*, by Po Chü-i (772–846). In fact, Shiki may even have had Yōkihi, the Emperor's love and the heroine of that poem, in mind, for in 1897 he had written a haiku in which the brilliant scarlet of the peony was associated with Yōkihi in a similar way:

Yōkihi no	the peony seems
neokigao naru	to think itself Yōkihi
botan kana	as she awakes (III, 62)

In the tanka, the emphatic rhythm imparted by the alliteration of "t" and "r," "k" and "m," and the assonance of "a," "e," and "i" impart a substantiality and heaviness foreign to the ideal of the classical tanka. This begins to change in the third and the fourth lines (the third line occupies a pivotal position, partaking of the character of both the first and second half of the poem), which constitute a noun phrase, typical of classical poems such as Teika's and also of many of Shiki's own later ones. The rich assonance of the last three lines, dominated by "o" and "a" with subcurrents of "i" and the alliteration of "n," lends a flow and melodiousness to the poem that brings it back to the diction of the classical tanka.

Saitō Mokichi's disciple Shibōta Minoru (b. 1904) expressed the belief that Shiki's point of departure for tanka such as this was the haiku of Buson and that his aim was to impart to the tanka a sensuousness it had hitherto lacked.[6] I would add, too, that the pictorial quality of the poem, with its juxtaposition of inner and outer scenes (bedchamber and garden), is also reminiscent of the haiku.

Other poems of this group possessed the same pictorial quality. Some even used haiku season words, such as *tama maku bashō* ("the tightly curled plaintain leaf" of summer):

ensaki ni	the plaintain at the veranda's edge
tama maku bashō	unfolds its coiled leaves,
tama tokete	its jewels,
goshaku no midori	and veils the water basin
chōzubachi o ōu	in five feet of green (VI, 118)

Introducing elements from foreign cultures was the last method Shiki offered for enriching the tanka. In *Letters to a Tanka Poet* #6 and #7, Shiki expressed his belief that the tanka could survive the onslaught of foreign cultures that characterized the Meiji period only through the acceptance of foreign influences. This put him in the seemingly paradoxical position of recommending surrender to the enemy as a way to survive its attack. He was acutely aware of this contradiction—indeed, his extremely vocal readership would not let him forget it.

In reply to a reader who had apparently expressed the conviction that if any changes were permitted in the tanka, "the ramparts of Japanese literature," the rest of the nation would come tumbling down, Shiki declared, in the sixth letter, that if the imperial anthologies were the ramparts of Japanese literature, they were most feeble ones. Such thin walls would collapse at the first cannon blast. He went on, employing the same imagery as his correspondent:

I have no intention of destroying the national poetry—I only want to strengthen the walls of Japanese literature a little. I wish with all my heart to make those walls so strong they will not even tremble when the hairy-faced foreigners fire their cannon and detonate their mines. . . . To consider the tanka as the foundation and ramparts of Japanese literature is like fighting with bows and arrows or swords and lance—it is out of place in the Meiji period. After all, paying out vast sums of money to foreign countries for warships and cannons is only to strengthen the Japanese nation. I want to keep importing the literary thought of foreign countries, which we can purchase for a song, to strengthen the ramparts of Japanese literature. In the tanka, I am also trying to destroy old patterns of thought and find new ones. Consequently, in vocabulary, too, I intend to use such words as are necessary, whether literary, colloquial, Chinese, or Western. (VII, 37)

In the seventh letter, continuing the same theme, Shiki wrote that the banality of the contemporary tanka stemmed from its limited subject matter, in turn the product of its restricted vocabulary. He therefore recommended the use of foreign words and foreign literary thought. Some people considered him a destroyer of Japanese literature because of these recommendations, but, he said, this was a basic misunderstanding:

Even if one writes a poem in Chinese, or a Western language, or, for that matter, Sanskrit, it is part of Japanese literature as long as its author is Japanese. A government organized by Japanese is a Japanese government, even if the ranks and their associated colors are modelled on the Chinese system and the uniforms are in the Chinese style [as was the case in Japan under the Taihō Code of 701]. Even if we win a war with warships bought from England and cannons from Germany [as in the Sino-Japanese War of 1894–1895], it is Japan's victory as long as the people using them are Japanese. . . . We cannot rely exclusively on Japanese things. If we were to delete Chinese loan words from our literature, including "horse," "plum blosssom," "butterfly," "chrysanthemum," "writing," and all the rest, what would be left? There would never have been a Japan if the Japanese had restricted themselves to native Japanese words, and Japanese literature will collapse if Japanese writers begin to do so now. (VII, 40)

Shiki concluded by declaring,

Any word which can express beauty is a proper word for tanka; there are no other tanka words. Whether Chinese or Western, all words that can be used literarily may be considered to belong to the vocabulary of the tanka. (VII, 41)

As the last sentence indicates again, Shiki's criterion was not the traditional requirements of the single genre, tanka, but the standards of a larger category that included and also transcended all genres—that is, literature (*bungaku*).

Most of the poems in *Ten Poems in a Hundred* illustrated Shiki's critical concerns; but some, while developing themes central to his writings, did not have such a direct theoretical application. For example,

"Byōchū Taikyō"	"Invalid Facing Mirror"
mukashi mishi	The man
omokage mo arazu	I used to meet in the mirror
otoroete	is no more.
kagami no hito no	Now I see a wasted face.
horohoro to naku	It dribbles tears. (VI, 138)

This is one of the earliest successful examples of Shiki's treatment of his physical deterioration in a tanka. It has the simplicity, honesty, and intimacy of tone that marks the best of his later poems.

Other poems of 1898 were less stark. Several described the dream world as a place of magic and beauty, a theme that appeared at intervals in his work from as early as *Scribblings* and continued through the journals of 1901 and 1902. A dream poem written while he was in China with the army, but dated 1898, was:

"Kinshū Jūgunchū Saku"   "In China with the Army"

haru samumi   In the spring chill,
hoko o makura ni   as I slept with sword by pillow,
neru yowa o   deep at night
kori no imōto zo   my little sister came to me
yume ni mietsuru   in dreams from home. (VI, 142)

Another tanka from the same year, while completely realistic, achieved a sense of mystery in its evocation of that space where memory and fantasy overlap. It was one of two entitled "Byōkan Ari Shashite Kōgai Ni Asobite" [Going into the Country by Carriage While Sick]:

sato o mite   saw the country
kaerishi yowa no   and returned—now deep at night
makuragami   I lie in bed and
na no hana saku no   fields of mustard flowers
me ni miyuru kamo   bloom before my eyes (VI, 154)

Again in 1898, he wrote a series of nine poems called *Byōchū Yume* [Dreams While Sick]. Perhaps the best was this:

ureshikumo   happily
noborishi Fuji no   I climbed Mt. Fuji and
itadaki ni   as my legs trembled
ashi wananakite   on its peak
yume samen to su   awoke (VI, 117, 181)

This poem has a certain ambiguity that enriches it, for one cannot tell if the poet's legs actually trembled in bed or were trembling in his dream, or both. Again we are in that space where reality and fantasy merge.

Considering Shiki's stress on the real in most of his criticism, his interest in dreams may seem rather inconsistent. If one considers his equally deep interest in depicting emotion, however, it is not so odd, for many of the dreams he recorded dealt with his most intense desires. The dreams show that Shiki's emphasis on objective reality was matched by his own absorption in the subjective processes of the mind. They explain the deep subjectivity one feels in even the most apparently objective and realistic poems of his last years. An early poem in this vein, again from the 1898 series "Dreams While Sick," was:

utatane no	wakened by pain
utata kurushiki	from a dream of pain
yume samete	I wipe the sweat
ase fuki oreba	and rose petals
bara no hana chiru	scatter (VI, 182)

This poem combines the dream theme with another that was to become central later, the juxtaposition of the dying Shiki with nature. The relation here between Shiki wiping his sweat and the roses scattering their petals seems rather forced and the ambiguity of the pivot word *kurushiki* ("painful," describing both the brief sleep and the speaker's dream) redundant rather than enriching.[7] Still, the poem is worth notice for the poet's effort to relate himself to the natural world around him.

In 1898, Shiki also wrote several groups of tanka—on the skylark, on baseball,[8] on going into the country, on silence, on dreams while sick (already mentioned), on thinking of his old home in the country, on flies, on the topic "If I could stand," on his garden. These may be seen as preparations for his later tanka sequences, taken up in Chapter 5.

In the group of tanka called "Waga Niwa" [My Garden], he was already beginning to make the intense and detailed observation of his immediate physical world that became typical of his later poems. One particularly lovely example was:

hitooke no	the bucket's water
mizu uchiyameba	poured out and gone,
horohoro to	drop by drop
tsuyu no tama chiru	dew drips like pearls
akikusa no hana	from the autumn flowers (VI, 195)

The images move from the bucket, to its water, to the water stopping its flow, then to the dripping of dew (actually not dew, but drops from the bucket), and finally to the autumn flowers (literally, "flowering autumn grasses"). Yet, in the Japanese, the autumn flowers are modified grammatically by all that comes before them; the poem (like many classical tanka) is an incomplete sentence, of which the autumn flowers are the predicateless subject. Therefore, the reader sees the flowers and all that has happened to them—their having been watered and then the water spilling over like dewdrops—included in one moment.

There is nothing especially striking, at first glance, in the way drops of water spill off flowers after they have been watered. It is the way in which this is seen, so that the entire process is described and at the same time held in stillness, that makes the poem compelling. The poem arrives at a balance between movement and stillness, process and finality. Yet—is it because of the artificiality of the unstated comparison of the drops of water from the bucket to dewdrops?—the poem, in the end, is not completely satisfying.

In many later poems, Shiki turned his eyes in much the same way, but with greater success, on seemingly insignificant phenomena. Most such poems were still lifes in words, describing his own observation of motionless objects, so it would have been possible for the total effect to be static. That the effect was, on the contrary, one of motion and vitality was due to the progression of images, an orderly movement that depicted the motion of the poet's observing eyes and graduating perception. In these poems, there was a process of transformation at work by which the ordinary becomes extraordinary—what one might call "the consecration of the everyday."

Several of the outstanding examples of this sort are from 1900, when Shiki decided that the complete harmonization of the haiku and the tanka and the creation of an "exalted thirty-one syllable haiku" was impractical. In the spring of that year, he wrote a friend that he was coming to realize there were differences between the haiku and the tanka other than their length. He now thought the haiku were more suited to objective expression and the tanka to subjective expression. Furthermore, he went on, he had supposed in 1898 that any scene appropriate to a haiku could be described equally well in thirty-one syllables, but experience had taught him how difficult it was to treat in a tanka the finely chiseled, minute, bright scenes so well suited to the haiku. He would not, however, go so far as to say, he concluded, that the themes of the two genres were mutually exclusive, for at least half were suited to both, and eight out of ten haiku subjects could also be used in tanka.

The diction of Shiki's tanka, which had previously possessed overtones of both the haiku and classical Chinese poetry, now moved even closer to one reminiscent of the *Manyōshū*. His vocabulary shifted from a liberal use of Chinese and Western loan-words to a predominant use of words of purely Japanese origin (*yamato-kotoba*), including both archaisms and neologisms. In an effort to avoid using any foreign words at all, he even translated Chinese loan-words (which are as Japanese as any Latin-origin English word is English) into cumbersome phrases he coined himself. *Dōbutsuen* ("zoo") became *kedamono no sono* ("wild beast garden"), as in the second of the following poems. *Kandankei* ("thermometer") became *samusa hakari* ("cold measure"). *Yūbin haitatsufu* ("mailman") became *fumikubar-ibito* ("mail distributing person").

Perhaps the earliest example of the *Manyōshū* influence on Shiki's diction was from the group of poems he wrote on baseball in 1898, the first of which was:

hisakata no	far away
Amerikabito no	under the skies of America
hajime ni shi	they began
bēsubōru wa	baseball—ah,
miredo akanu kamo	I could watch it forever! (VI, 178)

Here the phrase from classical tanka *hisakata no ame* ("under the far-reaching heavens"), which is included in *hisakata no Amerikabito* ("far away under the skies of America"), and the *Manyōshū* cliché *miredo akanu kamo* ("I could watch it forever") contrast oddly with the very contemporary subject matter. Other poems from 1900 were somewhat more successful. In the following poem about Ueno Zoo (Shiki could see the trees of Ueno Park from his window), the previously mentioned neologism "wild beast garden" appeared:

Ueno yama   as evening comes across
yū koekureba   Ueno Hill
mori kurami   the woods grow dark and
kedamono hoyuru   wild beasts howl in
kedamono no sono   the wild beast garden (VI, 260)

What was Shiki's purpose in using "wild beast garden" instead of the usual "zoo" in this poem? The rule that the last line of a tanka should be no more than seven syllables, a requirement satisfied by *kedamono no sono* but not *dōbutsuen*, might have had some influence but surely could not have been the determining factor for a poet of Shiki's skill. More important perhaps was the fact that *kedamono no sono*, with the alliteration and assonance of its last five syllables, and its similarity as a polysyllabic word to the other words in the poem, creates a unified sound. Were the flowing polysyllables of the native Japanese words suddenly broken by the introduction of a Chinese loan word, there would be a sense of disjunction which Shiki seems to have been avoiding.[9]

There was another motive, too. We know that Shiki believed the graceful, "feminine" tone of the imperial anthologies was not the only one suitable for the tanka and wished to introduce a more forceful tone. Strength is achieved in several ways in this poem. The repetition of the last two lines creates an emphatic quality, which would be lost if we shifted from "beasts" to "zoo." Furthermore, the picture of a gradually encroaching darkness out of which emerge the menacing cries of wild beasts would be vitiated by "zoo," which evokes the image of neatly caged animals. Thus, in using the neologism "wild beast garden," Shiki was concerned, it would seem, with creating first a flowing sound for his poem, and second an impression of strength.

In the sequence he wrote about dew upon the pine needles (also from 1900), one of his very best, the diction is the same. The word *aezu* and the use of *chiru* with *tama* in the second of the two poems that follow are variations on *Manyōshū* vocabulary: in the *Manyōshū*, *aezu* is presented in its archaic conjugation as *aenu*, and *chiru* is used to describe the spray from waves rather than dew. The word *chitsuyu* in the first poem, though having an archaic ring, was actually coined by Shiki.

matsu no ha no	on the pine needles,
hosoki hagoto ni	each of the slender needles,
oku tsuyu no	a dewdrop rests—
chitsuyu mo yura ni	a thousand pearls lie
tama mo koborezu	quivering, yet never fall

matsu no ha no	the tips of the pine
hasaki o hosomi	needles, so thin . . .
oku tsuyu no	no sooner
tamari mo aezu	does the dew collect
shiratama chiru mo	than white pearls scatter (VI, 320–21)

The flowing, one sentence structure of these poems tends to obscure the fact that, like many of Shiki's most interesting tanka, they are based on a tension between opposing elements. Here it is the tension between the drops falling and not falling. Both poems catch this in-between moment where two opposites exist side-by-side, neither overcoming the other—a moment of harmony-in-opposition. The following poem is perhaps the best of the entire sequence:

matsu no ha no	to every needle
ha goto ni musubu	of the needled pine it clings—
shiratsuyu no	the pearl white dew,
okite wa kobore	forming but to scatter,
koborete wa oku	scattering but to form (VI, 320)

The subject of this poem, the white dew (*shiratsuyu*) occupies the third line, which is, in terms of form, the poem's center. The third line serves as a fulcrum in terms of content as well, for what comes before it describes the dew in static terms (as clinging to every needle of the pine tree) while what comes after it describes the dew in active terms (as repeatedly forming and scattering). In other words, the first two lines speak of the dew that clings to the branches but in the last two lines we see that beneath that generalization about the drops of dew as a whole lies the infinitely changing reality of its continual breaking up and reforming, as one drop replaces another dropping from the branch. "White dew," then, means both "dew" in the general sense, and is a singular noun; and then also many specific

drops of dew, as a plural noun. (Japanese, with its paucity of plural/
singular distinctions can accommodate this ambiguity in a way that
English cannot.) Yet, this complexity is presented with extreme
simplicity, for the first two lines of the poem do nothing but indicate
that there is dew on the pine needles, and the last two lines do nothing
but describe the way the dew behaves.

Another way in which Shiki combined two oppositions in one tanka
was by basing a poem on the contrast between the indoors and
outdoors. In the following poem from 1900, the poet's indoor darkness
is contrasted to the tabi's whiteness outdoors, and the opposites are
again united through the medium of the poem's single, flowing
sentence structure. Here, however, because Shiki himself is in the
poem, there is an added dimension not found in the poem above on
the dew.

fuyugomoru	huddled up for winter
yamai no toko no	upon a bed of pain
garasudo no	I wipe the window
kumori nugueba	clear of frost and see
tabi hoseru miyu	tabi, hung out for drying (VI, 266)

Lying in bed in the depth of winter, Shiki wiped the frost off the
window (literally glass sliding door, but I used "window" in the
translation for poetic considerations), and saw tabi hanging up to dry
outside.[10] The poem's content is completely ordinary, one might even
say trivial. As in the previous poems, it is the way in which the poet
observes that gives his words significance, rather than what he
observes.

The poem's images proceed from inside to outside in one straight
line, from the dark warmth of his winter-wrapped bed, to the bright,
white coldness of the tabi outdoors. We go from winter (line 1) to the
"bed of pain" it enwraps (line 2), to the window that stands between
the inside and outside (line 3), to the frost on it being wiped away
(line 4 in the original, but line 3 and 4 in the translation), and then
finally to the white tabi drying in the bright winter sun (line 5). Inside
and outside are oppositions, of course, but the poem binds them by its
flowing, one-sentence structure and by the orderly progression, through

images, from one to the other. And as the glass stands between, a transparent boundary between inner and outer, and the joint between them, so the word *garasudo* itself is as near to the mathematical center of the poem (the third line) as it can be.

The poem, however, is not a mere formal triumph. Shiki himself is in the poem and this adds an emotional dimension and depth lacking in the poems discussed above. The reader knows that the cold winter day was sunny because the tabi are drying outside. One can imagine Shiki's feeling of delight at seeing the sun after the relative darkness of his confined sickroom. The emotion evoked by the poem is partly aesthetic—the beauty of the sudden appearance of the tabi, white and shining—and partly personal—the mingled delight and sadness of the invalid granted a momentary glimpse of a world he can no longer enter, a world symbolized by tabi, which are of use only to those who can walk. In other poems, Shiki described the sense of separation between himself and nature and the sad impossibility of bridging the gap; but here, while the images depict a gap, the syntax overcomes it. For a moment the chasm is bridged and his own sense of death's imminence transcended.

This poem is one of the earliest examples in the tanka of the personal, autobiographical quality of much of Shiki's later poetry. The persona created in these poems was not necessarily the faithful expression of the real Shiki. As comparison with the letters and with the private diary *Stray Notes While Lying On My Back* shows, the real Shiki was more absorbed in the physical details of existence, more hysterical, more irritable, more self-pitying, more despairing, than the poems reveal. Shiki the poet created a persona for his later poems and public diaries, a sort of second self, a refined version of his everyday self. This persona was an invalid whose contact with nature was confined to what he could see of his garden from his sickbed and whose intercourse with other human beings was limited to visitors to his home. His primary concern was death, in particular his own approaching death. Yet his obsession with this subject was expressed indirectly only, through his minute observation of nature. For example, the poem discussed above seems completely objective: we are told only that Shiki, lying in bed in the middle of winter, wiped the frost off a window and saw tabi drying outside. The observation is precise and detailed; we are told nothing about how it made him feel. Yet the poem acquires an intensity of feeling because the sense of his own imminent death underlies it, giving what seems a trivial observation tremendous importance. It is as if everyday objects came to have a heightened reality because each glimpse of one might be the last. This quality of heightened reality is what I mean by the phrase "the consecration of the everyday." Co-existent with this, was an acute sense of his own physical decay. The two came together in his later, most moving poems, as a poignant juxtaposition of his own decay with the vigor of nature, a juxtaposition which came to symbolize the opposition of life and death itself. The following poem, also from 1900, expressed this theme even more explicitly than the poem about the tabi:

"Gogatsu nanuka (taion   "May 7 (temperature 38.5°)"
sanjūhachido gobu)"

hashikiyashi   how like a lovely
otome ni nitaru   young girl it is,
kurenai no   this peony of scarlet red
botan no kage ni   whose shadow shades
utsuutsu nemuru   my fitful dreaming (VI, 312)

The youthful, virginal beauty of the peony is depicted next to the weak and suffering Shiki. Yet the basic contrast between the man's suffering and the flower's beauty is all but obliterated by the flowing, unbroken syntax and by the fact that the peony oversees the poet's dreams. One feels that the poet's dreams and his pain are softened by the nearness of the peony, as if the poet had given himself up wholly to the flower he likens to a young girl. Like a few other poems by Shiki, this seems to be a love poem addressed to a flower. Yet, beside this, there remain the stark factuality and matter-of-factness of the poem's title. The poem, while hinting at fantasy, never loses its sense of reality, bringing us again to that border between dream and reality where Shiki so often stood.

Although Shiki had given up harmonizing the haiku and the tanka by 1900 and after that his haiku and tanka styles diverged even more, there is another sense in which his work in the two forms during the last two years of his life came even closer than it had been, for in both the theme of his own death and parting from this world became central. It would be of interest to examine the haiku and the tanka of these years in order to see how the different requirements of the two forms made Shiki express the same theme in different ways. Because of the artificial distinctions maintained between the haiku and the tanka even now, however, it seems even more important to point out first the underlying unity of theme in them. Accordingly, in the next section, I will consider Shiki's later haiku and tanka together.

Haiku and Tanka: 1900–1902

The best of Shiki's later poems, whether haiku or tanka, are descriptions of nature in the sketch from life style. Usually no attempt is made to distinguish between the different kinds of poems within this one category.[11] There is in fact, however, a crucial distinction to be made, between those poems which simply describe nature and those which, while describing nature, have as their subject the relation between the poet himself and nature. It is in the latter that Shiki worked out his relation to the world as he prepared to leave it, moved from resistance to his fate to a kind of resignation that suggests a final spiritual transcendence and reconciliation.

Two examples of the first type of poem—pure natural description, in which the poet himself does not figure—are these haiku from 1900 and 1902:

fuji no hana   wisteria plumes
nagōshite ame   sweep the earth, and soon
furan to su   the rains will fall (III, 334)

kuroki made ni   purple unto
murasaki fukaki   blackness:
budō kana   grapes! (III, 473)

The first poem vividly conveys the pregnant dampness of early summer heat in Japan through the full, heavy plumes of the wisteria. The second, with its repeated ''k'' sounds, is an emphatic declaration of the purpleness, a celebration of a natural beauty that particularly impressed Shiki. The center of the first poem is the wisteria and the

summer; of the second, the color of the grapes. In neither do we feel
the personal presence of the poet himself.

Shiki wrote tanka as well as haiku of pure natural description. Two
examples, the first already discussed in the previous chapter, are:

matsu no ha no	on the pine needles
hosoki hagoto ni	each of the slender needles
oku tsuyu no	a dewdrop rests—
chitsuyu mo yura ni	a thousand pearls lie
tama mo koborezu	quivering yet never fall (VI, 320)
kurenai no	two feet tall,
nishaku nobitaru	the crimson-budded roses,
bara no me no	their young thorns
hari yawaraka ni	tender in
harusame no furu	the soft spring rain (VI, 309)

There was also a different sort of poem, however, in which the
poet's presence was implied or overtly stated. The effectiveness of the
first type of poem, the objective description of nature, comes solely
from the beauty of the description itself, but that of the poems in
which the poet himself figures comes from the relationship between
the poet and the natural beauty he is observing. In the poems which
express this relationship least ambiguously, the poet and nature are
depicted in simple juxtaposition, and nature is something which
consoles him by its mere existence. For example, in 1900 Shiki wrote
this tanka as part of a sequence on some peonies he had received:

yami fuseru	to where I lie,
waga makurabe ni	sick upon my bed,
hakobikuru	they brought for me
hachi no botan no	these potted peonies . . .
hana yure yamazu	their petals' trembling never ends (VI, 306)

Peonies were Shiki's favorite flower, and here one feels that he
takes their delicate trembling as a way of speaking to him.

A poem which differs in subject but, similarly, expresses the theme
of nature as consolation is this haiku of 1902 from *Stray Notes While
Lying On My Back*:

byōshō no	I thought I felt
ware ni tsuyu chiru	a dewdrop on me
omoi ari	as I lay in bed (III, 469; XI, 507)

The headnote of this poem explains that Shiki had been given a scroll depicting certain flowers and grasses and had been looking at it the entire day. (The scroll was actually not given, but, unknown to Shiki, only lent to him, to be returned after his death.) The sickbed was a place of suffering and decay, but suddenly, inspired by the versimilitude of the scroll, the poet feels himself in the world of the scroll, a flower sprinkled by dew.

Nature's influence on the poet is not always as benevolent and life-enhancing as in this poem. For example, this tanka from the ten-poem sequence in *A Drop of Ink* entitled "I can't help taking up my brush":

yamu ware o	as if to cheer me
nagusamegao ni	on my bed of pain,
hirakitaru	the peony spreads
botan no hana o	its petals wide and
mireba kanashi mo	seeing this I grieve (VI, 411)

Similarly, in this tanka of 1902, part of a series of six on a bonsai he received, the flower's beauty only increases the poet's sense of loneliness:

makurabe ni	when to my pillow
tomonaki toki wa	no friend comes
hachiue no	I lie alone,
ume ni mukaite	turned to face
hitori fushi ori	the potted plum (VI, 425)[12]

He may try to make the plum blossoms substitute for his absent friends, but he is still alone. The focus of the poem, in short, is not the beauty of the flowers, but the poet's own emotion.

In a haiku from a sequence on the same bonsai, the loneliness arises from the scattering of the flowers as well as the poet's solitude:

kōbai no   crimson plum blossoms
chirinu sabishiki   scattered over the loneliness
makura moto   of the bed . . . (III, 446)

The word *sabishiki*, "lonely," comes exactly between *chirinu*, "scattered," and *makura moto*, "by the bed," and grammatically speaking, it is both the scattering of the blossoms and the bed (a synecdochic trope for the poet) which are lonely. The word "lonely," then, expresses the poet's sense of identification with the flower, in whose evanescence Shiki saw mirrored the brevity of his own life. The plum blossoms consoled because they were like him, were close to him; but at the same time, they intensified his sadness about his own mortality. Many poems which depict Shiki in relation to nature express this complex of emotion. Another example is from the same haiku sequence,

kōbai no   fallen petals of
rakka o tsumamu   the crimson plum I pluck
tatami kana   from the tatami (III, 446)

Here one feels the poet's love of the bonsai's beauty and his solitude, as in the previous poem, but also a new element, that of boredom.

In the sequence of which this poem is part, Shiki fluctuates between seeing the bonsai as separate from himself and as part of himself, with all the complexity of emotions that that implies. Still, even when he sees himself as separate from the bonsai, the relation is an intimate one. However, Shiki also wrote poems which presupposed an impassable distance and separation, an alienation, from nature. In some of these, the sense of separation was expressed as a simple juxtaposition of opposites. One example is the first verse of the 1901 tanka sequence on the wisteria (discussed as a sequence in Chapter 5), which says only that the distance between the poet and the wisteria is too great for the wisteria to reach the tatami where he lies:

kame ni sasu   wisteria
fuji no hanabusa   in the vase
mijikakereba   so short
tatami no ue ni   it doesn't touch
todokazarikeri   the floor (XI, 175; VI, 408)

In this poem, the poet is observing at one and the same time two separate entities, himself and the flower, and the poem's center is the separation between them. A similar, but earlier, poem is the second one from the 1896 haiku sequence on the snow, discussed in Chapter 2:

> ikutabi mo   again and again
> yuki no fukasa o   I ask how high
> tazunekeri   the snow is

This, too, evokes the simultaneous existence of two opposites, the poet himself and the snow, one dying and diminishing, one increasing and alive. It was, however, written five years before the wisteria sequence, and the attitude it implies toward the natural world is one of almost childish enthusiasm, quite different from the elegaic tone and, then, the detached tone of the poems of 1901 and 1902.

In many of the tanka of 1901 and 1902, Shiki, resigned to his own death, expressed a loving tenderness for this world, as though it were already part of his own past. As Ōoka Makoto has written, these poems are epitaphs for each flower they describe.[13]

In the first two tanka from the sequence of May 4 in *A Drop of Ink,* Shiki linked spring's end to his own death:

> Saogami no   ah, sad to part
> wakare kanashi mo   from Lady Sao . . .
> kon haru ni   in the spring to come
> futatabi awan   it will not be me
> ware naranaku ni   who meets her again[14]

> ichihatsu no   the wall iris
> hana saki-idete   opens its buds:
> waga me ni wa   before my eyes
> kotoshi bakari no   the last spring
> haru yukan to su   begins to fade

In the sixth poem of the same sequence, Shiki expressed the belief that he would be dead by the coming autumn:

yūgao no	I dream of making
tana tsukuran to	a trellis for moonflowers
omoedomo	to climb,
aki machigatenu	but oh my life, that will not
waga inochi kamo	bear the wait till autumn! (XI, 180)

It was hardly surprising that the end of spring might suggest to Shiki the end of his own life, and the parting from spring his parting from this world. Nature came to stand for life itself, and the poet for mortality and death. In his final haiku, in fact, Shiki even spoke of himself as a Buddha, that is, one already dead.

The closer Shiki came to death, the stronger became his sense of separation from nature and of alienation from the human world. In the diaries, his sense of alienation was most often expressed in subjective tones of petulance and self-pity, sometimes relieved by irony. Shiki's last writings, however, were not in prose, but in poetry, specifically haiku. In the three haiku he wrote just hours before his death, he abandoned the attachment to this world felt in earlier poems and moved to resignation and a final transcendence.

The first of these poems was:

hechima saite	the gourd flowers bloom,
tan no tsumarishi	but look—here lies
hotoke kana	a phlegm-stuffed Buddha! (III, 473)

Here, the poet is no longer characterized as a sick man but as a dead man, and the separation between himself and the world he observes has become complete and final. In the poems discussed above, Shiki either identified with nature (as in the poems on the plum bonsai) or else, while feeling separate from it, lamented the separation. There was always a sense that he was trying to overcome the distance between himself and the beauty he observed, trying to hang onto life, or, at least, regretting the leaving of it.

The juice of the gourd, gathered from the plant before it bloomed, was used to relieve coughing such as Shiki's. However, as his condition became past remedy, the juice had become useless and the flowers allowed to come into bloom. The blooming of the flowers, lovely in itself, has a sinister meaning, for it signifies the hopelessness of Shiki's

condition, implies his death. Living flowers mean a dying Shiki—
again two opposites, held at once in the mind.[15]

In the next two of the three final haiku, the poet says that even if
there were gourd water it would not help. In other words, he is
already dead and there can be no turning back to life:

tan itto	a quart of phlegm—
hechima no mizu mo	even gourd water
ma ni awazu	couldn't mop it up (III, 473)

ototoi no	they didn't gather
hechima no mizu mo	gourd water
torazariki	day before yesterday either (III, 473)

With the negatives ("can't," "didn't") of these poems, Shiki was
declaring the end of his relation to this world. He had left behind the
"infinite ambition" of his youth for the "zero wish" of Enlightenment.

Chapter Four

Prose: "The Little Garden Is My Universe"

History of Sketch from Life Prose

Shiki, as related in Chapter 1, had given up his original ambition of becoming a novelist and turned to poetry in 1892, after Kōda Rohan's cool reception of his novella, *The Capital by Moonlight*. In 1898, however, when the offices of *Hototogisu* moved from Matsuyama to Tokyo and Takahama Kyoshi became the editor, Shiki turned back to prose in addition to his poetry. Shiki's extension of sketch from life prose was a natural development, given the fact that he had declared from the beginning of his career that his primary commitment was to literature rather than to any single genre. It was the success of *Hototogisu*[1] that enabled him to broaden its scope to include other forms besides the haiku—tanka, new-style verse, literary and art criticism, as well as short prose essays.

Shiki's first essay in the new style was *Shōen no Ki* [Record of the Little Garden], published in October 1898. In the following year he published *Kumo no Nikki* [Cloud Diary], a description of the clouds passing through the winter sky, and *Natsu no Yo no Oto* [Sounds of a Summer Night], about the sounds he heard on a summer night from eight in the evening until two in the morning. Others of his more famous essays were *Meshi Matsu Aida* [Waiting for Lunch, 1899], the title of which speaks for itself, and *Koi* [Love, 1899], a vindication of the Tokugawa period heroine Yaoya Oshichi, whose passion led her to set a fire that destroyed part of Edo.

Shiki's final essay, written four days before his death, was *Kugatsu Jūyokka no Asa* [The Morning of September 14]. Here, in spite of pain so great that he could not write and had to dictate the essay (to Kyoshi), he described his own physical and mental state and the gourd flowers, autumn grasses and other sights of his garden.

While many of his essays were about his garden, many were not. In *Sake* [Sake, 1899], he related how he had gotten drunk on a liter of cheap sake and fallen asleep the night before a trigonometry examination in college and then failed the examination. *Tabi* [Travel, 1899] was another reminiscence of his younger and healthier days. *Yamai* [Sickness, 1899] was about his return from China and all that had ensued until he was hospitalized in Kobe. *Kudamono* [Fruit, 1901] was a disquisition on fruit, of which he was inordinately fond.

Other essays told of the fantasies he had while lying in bed. Chief among these was the chilling *Rampu no Kage* [The Lamp's Shadow, 1900] in which, as he lay alone one night, the shadow cast by the lamp suggested to him various faces, including a goblin, a Western child, a young girl, a festival mask, a monkey mask, Jesus Christ, a tuberculosis patient, and finally, a dead man. In *Yume* [A Dream, 1899], only one paragraph long, he told of a dream in which cherry blossoms were scattering over a hillside and he met a beautiful woman. In *Hatsuyume* [First Dream, 1901], he dreamt of visiting his friends' homes one by one and even of returning to his birthplace in Matsuyama. In the humorous and poignant *Shigo* [After Death, 1901], he imagined various ways to dispose of his body after death— in a coffin, buried under the earth, cremation, or being lowered into the ocean; but none pleased him and he finally admitted he would like to become a star.

In still other essays, he recorded the occasions when he went on excursions by rickshaw. *Shajō Shoken* [Sights from a Rickshaw, 1898] told of what he saw when he went out into the countryside. In the imaginative and humorous *Kumade to Chōchin* [Rakes and Lanterns, 1899], he related a visit to Oka Fumoto (1871–1951) in early winter. On the way home he had seen many people carrying good luck rakes of varying sizes and prices bought at one of the seasonal *tori no ichi*[2] festivals, and had amused himself by speculating about the purchasers on the basis of the kind of rakes each had bought. *Shajō no Shunkō* [Spring Scenes from a Rickshaw, 1900] told of a call paid on Itō Sachio in the spring.

There were also humorous accounts of the gatherings of his disciples such as *Yumiso Kai* [Citron Miso Society, 1899]. All told, between 1898 and 1902, Shiki published twenty-seven short essays in the new style in *Hototogisu*; the longest was ten pages and most were shorter. In addition, in 1900–1901 he solicited through its pages diaries to be called *Ichinichi Kiji* [Record of a Day] and published the best entries in six consecutive issues.

Besides his own essays, Shiki wrote several theoretical essays about sketch from life prose and also organized the *Yama Kai* [Mountain Society],[3] whose members met periodically at his sick bed to read their work aloud and receive his criticisms. Kyoshi remarked with some petulance in *Shiki Koji to Yo* [Shiki and I, 1915] that a piece adversely criticized by Shiki at one of these gatherings had little chance of being published in *Hototogisu*; but he did admit that the meetings were a good stimulus to write and thus perpetuate the magazine. The members, in addition to Kyoshi and Shiki, included many of Shiki's disciples in the haiku and tanka: Kawahigashi Hekigotō, Sakamoto Shihōda (1873–1917), Matsuse Seisei (1869–1938), Samukawa Sokotsu, Itō Sachio, Satō Kōroku (1874–1949), Oka Fumoto, and Natsume Sōseki.

The first anthology of prose by Shiki and his disciples was entitled *Kangyokushū* [Collection of Beautiful Jewels, 2 vol., 1900–1901] and edited by Kyoshi. In 1900, Kyoshi also edited *Sunkōshū* [Bits of Red Collection]. After Shiki's death, more anthologies appeared: in 1903, *Shaseibunshū* [Collection of Sketch from Life Prose], edited by Kyoshi; in 1906, *Hotategai* [Scallop], edited by Kyoshi and Sakamoto Shihōta; in 1907, *Zoku Shaseibunshū* [Sequel to Collection of Sketch from Life Prose], edited by Shihōta; in 1908, *Shin Shaseibun* [New Sketch from Life Prose], edited by Kyoshi. After this, the anthologies veered more toward works by single authors, such as Kyoshi's collection of short stories, *Keitō* [*Cockscombs*, 1908].

According to Kyoshi, Shiki considered his work in prose to be even more revolutionary than that in poetry. He said that while his work in haiku had been more of a revival than a revolution, with sketch from life prose he and his friends had created something really new. Kyoshi gives no explanation for this remark, but some idea of what Shiki meant may be gleaned from remarks he made in passing about the difference between the short essays he and his colleagues published in *Hototogisu* and the style of the Meiji novel in the article *Hototogisu*

Daiyonkan Daiichigo no Hajime ni [For the Beginning of *Hototogisu*, Vol. IV, No. 1, 1900]. He wrote that since realistic prose was then extremely popular and novels were usually written realistically, there might seem to be nothing unusual in the short realistic essays which *Hototogisu* was then publishing. Such essays did differ, however, from realistic novels in that they made any subject in the human or natural worlds the object of a single unified work. Furthermore, the author's aim was to make the subject, whether it was a static scene or a series of events in time, appear before one's eyes as soon as one read the words, so that one felt one was seeing and touching the thing itself, and to do this without becoming verbose or boring the reader.

Shiki's point seems to have been that the prose sketch from life was freer in subject matter than the realistic novel, dealing with natural phenomena as well as human affairs, and that as a style it aimed for an effect of greater visual immediacy. Both points seem unexceptionable, but still leave open the question of how the prose sketch from life differed from *haibun* (haiku-style prose), a genre that dated from the Tokugawa period. There was in fact a tendency to see essays in the sketch from life as a form of haiku-style prose. For example, in 1905 *Record of the Little Garden* and *Cloud Diary* as well as an essay each by Kyoshi and Hekigotō were included in a collection entitled *Meiji Haibunshū* [Collection of Meiji Period Haiki-Style Prose].

Shiki's earliest sketch from life prose, typified by *Record of the Little Garden,* was quite close to haiku-style prose in several ways. The haiku-style prose of the Tokugawa period, as written by Matsuo Bashō and others, was characterized by an elliptical, highly condensed style, literary allusions to both Chinese and Japanese authors, the inclusion of haiku poems, and the avoidance of both extended fantasy and logical or philosophical argument. It usually had a light tone, often deepened by an underlying seriousness. *Record of the Little Garden* has many of these traits, as will be shown later.

However, as Shiki continued to write sketch from life essays, he moved farther away from haiku-style prose and closer to a new form. The tone of the relatively late *After Death,* for example, retains the same mixture of humor and poignance as the earlier essays, but in many other ways it differs from haiku-style prose: its language is lucid, almost to the point of repetition; there are no literary allusions and no poems; the subject is Shiki's own fantasies about how to have his body disposed of after death; and these ruminations are presented within the framework of a quasi-logical disquisition on human attitudes toward death. In addition, there is an interest in the intricate involutions of his own thoughts that is quite different from Bashō or any Tokugawa-period writer.

Historically the sketch from life movement represents a distinct stage in the development of modern prose fiction, coming midway between the Meiji period realistic novel and the naturalists of the late Meiji and Taishō periods. The realistic novel as developed by Tsubouchi Shōyō and Futabatei Shimei preceded Shiki's movement; the naturalist movement, heralded by Tayama Katai (1871–1930), began after Shiki's death, in about 1908.

The sketch from life movement flourished as a movement only as long as *Hototogisu* was under Kyoshi's control and even then in the later Meiji period only. It was then seen as the only noteworthy rival to naturalism, although never a serious one. Yet, in spite of this, it can be argued persuasively that modern realistic prose was brought into being by the writers who followed in Shiki's wake rather than by the naturalists.[4] The most outstanding example of an influential modern novelist whose style was greatly influenced by the sketch from life movement is Natsume Sōseki, particularly in his early novels such as *Wagahai wa neko de aru* [I Am a Cat, 1905–1907] and *Kusa Makura* [Pillow of Grass, 1906]. Nagatsuka Takashi's (1879–1915) modern classic, the novel *Tsuchi* [Earth, 1912] also came out of the sketch from life movement, as did lesser works by Kyoshi and Itō Sachio. Sōseki passed on some of the sketch from life influence to his own disciples Terada Torahiko (1878–1935), Suzuki Miekichi (1882–1936) and Nogami Yaeko (b. 1885), all of whom published early works in *Hototogisu*. It is difficult to document influences beyond this, because the forms in which the influence of Shiki's sketch from life has been most important—the novel and short story—are different from the form in which Shiki himself worked. Nevertheless, the extent to which it has left a lasting imprint on modern Japanese literature is hinted at by such statements as Shiga Naoya's (1883–1971) that he had liked Shiki's essays in *Hototogisu* very much and may have been influenced by them, and by Shiba Ryōtarō's assertion that modern prose begins with Shiki.[5]

Sketch from Life Essays

The Mountain Society derived its name from Shiki's teaching that every prose passage should have a mountain; by this he meant a climax. The beginning should be low, like the foot of Mt. Fuji; it should gradually ascend and reach a peak, and from there gradually descend.

Shiki's theoretical statements on sketch from life prose were not usually any more complicated than his doctrine of the mountain. The most extended formulation of his views was in the essay *Jojibun* [Descriptive Prose, 1900].[6] Others were made in the notes accompanying the publication of the *Record of a Day* diaries, in *For the Beginning of Hototogisu, Vol. IV, No. 1*, and in *A Sixfoot Sickbed* (entry of June 26), although the latter was a discussion of the sketch from life style in general.

In *Descriptive Prose*, Shiki emphasized the need for selection in prose, as he had in poetry:

If one makes central the most beautiful and moving, the scene comes alive of itself. And the most beautiful and moving part is not always large, conspicuous or essential. Often it is obscure, as though half-hidden in shadows. A single red camellia discovered amidst the obscure and frightening darkness of a forest is extremely beautiful and creates a feeling of joy. One can make the camellia the center of the composition then, but this does not necessarily mean describing it in detail. If you describe the dim, fearful aspect of the forest in rather complete detail and then merely indicate the red camellia, a strong feeling can be conveyed to the reader by a single word.

At the beginning of the same essay, he wrote that descriptive prose was a method of depicting things from the natural and human worlds in "interesting prose." After differentiating it from archaic or elegant prose, ornamental prose and prose which skillfully expressed the author's ideals, he went on further to give this prescription for it.

When one sees a certain scene or human happening and thinks it interesting, and wants to put it into words which will make the reader feel the same interest as oneself, one should not employ verbal decoration or exaggeration but should simply depict the thing itself as it is, as one sees it.

He then gave an example of a very general description of the sea coast at Suma. This, he said, he found uninteresting, and proceeded to present two more versions of it, each time adding more concrete details, and in the final version putting it in the first person.

After the description of Suma, Shiki gave as an example a sketch of a regional festival in which the writer told all he knew about it, but gave no sense of its atmosphere. Again, the second version was more specific, beginning "this morning" and shifting to the first person.

Shiki then went on to give examples of good beginnings for sketch from life essays. His first example concerned an essay about a winter ritual in which people dress in white kimonos and go about from house to house pouring cold water over themselves in order to purify body and spirit. "The winter bathing ritual in this locality is . . . ," he said, would not be a good beginning. Something more specific and personal would be better, such as "I had set out that night hoping to see the winter bathing ritual. The moon was clear and the wind blew as though piercing my body," with the author waiting a long time in the cold, becoming more and more uneasy, until finally a figure in a white kimono appeared, who was to perform the ritual.

A comparison of the various original and revised versions in *Descriptive Prose* reveals more about Shiki's conception of sketch from life prose. The most obvious changes are in the addition of concrete details and the shifting of the point of view from the third-person general to the first-person specific, so that everything is seen through the author's eyes. Both characteristics follow from the definition of descriptive prose that Shiki gave at the beginning of the essay, and both seem fairly obvious rules for good descriptive writing. The stylistic tradition in which most young Meiji writers had been trained, however, made these rules quite difficult to follow, even for Shiki himself. In this essay, written two years after he first began to publish sketches from life in prose, he does quite well; but his first sketch from life, *Record of the Little Garden,* is not quite so faithful to his own ideals.

How Shiki's sketch from life prose developed is well illustrated by *Record of the Little Garden,* his earliest such essay and one of the most interesting:[7]

I have a little garden, eighty yards square. It is on the south side of the house; the cryptomeria of Ueno are visible beyond the fence. Here on the outskirts of the city the houses are far apart, and so there is nothing to obstruct my view of the blue sky, stretching out beyond the garden with the clouds' goings and the birds soaring high. When I first moved here, it seemed no more than the remains of a bamboo grove, for there was only bare ground with neither grass nor trees. But then the landlord planted three small pines, and it took on a bit more shape, and when to these were added the rose seedlings given us by the old lady next door, I was often moved to poetry by its four or five flowers. One year I was in Shantung with the army. On the way back I fell ill and unexpectedly had to spend half a year at Suma and my birthplace. When I returned to my home here, it was near the end of autumn. The garden was far more disordered than the year before, and twisted stalks of white chrysanthemums were blooming here and there in disarray. When I faced this scene and quietly thought of yesterday, a myriad of feelings filled my heart, and my body, which had barely managed to return intact, found its failing health vanquished by delight. Close to tears, I found myself reciting "My garden overgrown."[8] I had never thought that such common flowers, such a cramped garden could move one so much. And now that my illness has worsened to the point that I can neither stand up nor go outdoors, the little garden is my universe and its plants and flowers have become the sole material for my poems. All that makes me think this life somewhat better than languishing at a prison window is the existence of this little plot of land and its quantity of lovely flowers.

The next year, on a day when spring's warmth was beginning to gather, and the voices of the birds could be heard clear and bright, I opened the window of the sick room and dragging myself close to the veranda, let my eyes, weary from reading, stray. The plants stirred with life, fresh and vivid, even within that space no larger than the palm of a hand, and even the cool penetration of the still slightly chill breeze into the gaps of my robe felt delightful. The vigor and strength of the clover bush (which I am told we also received from the old lady next door) as it put forth buds of green made me look forward to its autumn colors. I often spent the day, from past noon until dusk fell on the pasania tree, in a trance, looking at nothing in particular, as though drunk, as though all my strength were spent.

I who until then had been tormented and thoroughly weakened by cold and disease, felt like a child given new life, and as though from then on I would grow sturdy together with the buds of clover. Just then a yellow butterfly came flying by and as I watched it forage among the flowers in the hedge, my soul began to move out to it as though by instinct. Together we visited the flowers, searched out fragrances, and alit in the buds of things. Just as I thought to rest my wings for a moment, it crossed over the low cryptomeria hedge and circled the neighboring garden and again came wheeling back to flutter in the pine tops and over the water basin. Then, blown off by a gust of wind, it soared high and away. By the time it was hidden by the roof across the way, I was beside myself, lost in ecstasy. Suddenly coming to my senses, I noticed that I was feverish and feeling rather unwell. I came indoors, closed the paper sliding door, and pulled the quilt over me; yet in true reality I was dancing madly with the butterfly, now flown off over a broad, boundless plain. In the midst of my dancing, several hundred butterflies gathered from somewhere, and as I gazed at them playing I realized that what seemed butterflies were all little children of the gods. To the sound of music echoing from the sky, they danced and soared and flew away and I, determined not to be left behind, stepped without caring upon the thorns and goose grass. I danced through them until I realized that I had gone and fallen into a river. I woke up to find my underkimono soaked through with sweat and my temperature gone up to perhaps 102 degrees.[9]

When the lotus grass flowers[10] have passed their peak, and the hototogisu visits the sky overhead, the red roses and the white roses come into full bloom. There is some reward in watching their lovely colors, but the real beauty of my little garden is only revealed when the bush clover and the silver grass reach their peak. Compared with last year, the bush clover has been full of strength this year; even the way its branches sprawled luxuriantly at the summer's beginning seemed to hold promise for later, and the color of its leaves, unlike last year's yellowish hue, is a deep, deep green. On clear days, I several times had a chair placed nearby and managing to reach it with someone's help, would amuse myself by removing the small insects that foraged among the buds. From late August, when the Chinese bellflowers and the pinks went to seed, and there were only a few morning glories left, one or two of the long-awaited bush clover began to open. With delight enough to make me fly, I ticked them off in anticipation . . . four the next day, eight the day after that, ten days later perhaps a thousand—Then, one night a severe storm wind blew. The next morning, I woke from uneasy dreams to the sun high in the sky and loud voices in the garden. Anxiously,

I crawled outside to ask what was going on. The branches of the bush clover, until now so luxuriant, had virtually all given way. Shocked and downcast, I wondered what to do; but nothing could be done. Had I known this might happen, I lamented foolishly, I would have staked up each branch. Even the late autumn wind that blew the tiles down last year did not do this—perhaps the direction of this year's blast was bad for the bush clover? The day was cloudless with a touch of autumn in the air; I had the chair I spoke of earlier placed in the garden and filling a bucket and metal basin with water, I washed the mud off those bush clover that had escaped damage; but all it did was make my legs hurt more, and in the end the buds on the tips of the muddied clover rotted without blooming. The only things in the garden left unharmed were the pine trees and the silver grass.

Last spring—I think it was shortly after the Equinox—I was given several bags of flower seeds by Ōgai[11] and planted them at once; but except for the zinnias, nothing came up. I had wanted the amaranths especially and regretted them very much. This summer, I don't know where from, some strange buds appeared. Since they were about where I had planted the amaranth seeds last year, I thought it must be them, so I put up bamboo stakes and nurtured them carefully and after all, as I thought, the earliest leaves showed some red. I was so delighted that I uprooted the portulaca nearby, and when the amaranths had finally become about a foot high, and the autumn windstorms came, I worried only about them. But contrary to expectations, it was the bush clover that gave way and the amaranths were only bent a little. I helped them up and tied them to bamboo stakes and now they've safely reached two feet. Though they are thin and frail, their fiery red leaves dangle down in the most lovely way. Two or three days later, about four fat cockscombs, a present from the house across the way, were planted next to them. Was it the following day? In the early morning, I heard someone knock at the back door. When it was opened, there was Fusetsu, come carrying a large amaranth. Dampened by the morning fog, he planted it with his own hands before leaving.

Overwhelmed by autumn with its splendid and colorful cockscombs and amaranths, the bush clover has already begun to scatter, a poignant sight. The old lady next door who gave us roses, bush clover, silver grass and Chinese bellflowers and helped in the creation of my little paradise later moved elsewhere. This year, I heard, she passed on, showing the way to the autumn wind.

gotegote to	a jumble of
kusabana ueshi	flowers planted—
koniwa kana	see, the little garden! (XII, 235–39)

Most of Shiki's prose from 1900 to 1902 was written in the colloquial, but in 1898 he still used the literary language, as he does in this essay. As he himself was to point out two years later in *Descriptive Prose*, the colloquial was better suited to the sketch from life. *Record of the Little Garden* is written in the ornate style that was so easy to fall into when using the literary language. Such clichés as "a myriad of feelings filled my heart," and "no better than languishing at a prison window"; such exaggerated sentences as "I often spent the day . . . in a trance, looking at nothing in particular, as though drunk, as though all my strength were spent"; the author breaking into Chinese poetry to express deep feeling just as a character in opera, carried away by emotion, breaks into song; the fanciful flight with the butterflies—all are examples of the stylistic affectations that Shiki was to renounce by 1900. In the latter part of the essay, however, from the paragraph beginning "When the lotus flowers have passed their peak," the style becomes more matter-of-fact. The overt expressions of emotion in the first part of the essay give way to specific "as is" description of the flowers and Shiki's relation to them. The image of Shiki washing the mud off the bush clover with paternal solicitude, for example, says more about his feeling for the garden than all his earlier expressions of delight. With this change in style, the mood too shifts from one inclined to fancy to one firmly rooted in concrete reality. We can see Shiki working toward the unadorned colloquial language and the reliance on fact that characterized his later sketch from life essays and the diaries of 1901–1902.

The structural unity of the piece is marred somewhat by the shift in mood and style described above, but two factors overcome the effects of this and make the essay cohere: the old lady, and Shiki's feeling for the garden. The main body of the essay (it starts with the second paragraph: "The next year, on a day when spring's warmth . . .") opens with the blooming of the bush clover and closes with their decline as summer gives way to autumn. Parallel to this is the old lady's transition from life-giving benefactress of the garden to her death, which is phrased (using a poetic cliché) as a return to nature: "she passed on, showing the way to the autumn wind." The old lady is more than an old lady; perhaps she personified the fruitfulness of spring and summer to Shiki, and when they pass, so does she. (There is something particularly noble and right in a person of years being a giver of new life.)

Just as there is no gap between the old lady and the nature to which she returns, so Shiki feels none between his own human world and that of nature, as symbolized by the garden. He feels as passionately about the flowers in his garden as if they were his children. When the bush clover break in the storm, he goes out to bathe the mud off those that have escaped damage; at other times he plucks the tiny insects from them as one might groom a favorite pet.

The essay's theme is the sense of life given Shiki by the growing things in his garden, a theme that was also central to his poetry from 1897 on. As spring approaches and the garden starts to come alive, he writes, "I who until then had been tormented and thoroughly weakened by cold and disease, felt like a child given new life, and as though from then on I would grow sturdy together with the buds of clover." The emotion expressed explicitly here, is implicit in the already-discussed haiku entitled "Before the Garden": "cockscombs . . ./must be 14,/or 15."

The essay is also typical of Shiki in that he writes of seemingly trivial and mundane matters—a little garden, a few flowers and plants, an insignificant old lady, and a few friends—in such a way that they suggest more than themselves. Like all of Shiki's best writing, it is imbued with a consciousness of the coexistence of life and death. In addition, it both shows what Shiki's sketch from life prose style began as and what it would become. There are a few sketch from life essays which are more successful, such as *After Death* or *The Lamp's Shadow*, and I would have liked to have space to quote from both here; but *Record of the Little Garden* is more important than either for an understanding of the development of Shiki as a writer. In any case, the true culmination of Shiki's sketch from life prose was not in the essays at all but in the diaries of 1901 and 1902.

Chapter Five

Diaries: "I Feel the Pain and See the Beauty"

The Diaries as Uta-Nikki: Prosaic Poetry and Poetic Prose

By the time he came to write *A Drop of Ink*, *A Sixfoot Sickbed* and *Stray Notes While Lying On My Back*, Shiki had perfected his prose style. It had an ease, a grace, a simplicity that are rare in any literature. Unfortunately, it is not possible to illustrate such characteristics except by reference to the Japanese originals. Here I would like instead to discuss how Shiki combined his sketch from life prose with poetic elements and in so doing created a modern form of the poetic diary.

Shiki's earliest sketch from life essay, *Record of the Little Garden*, had several poetic elements—the quotation from the Chinese poet T'ao Ch'ien, the flight of fancy about the butterflies, the haiku at the end, the haiku map of the garden itself. It and other essays of Shiki's, as mentioned already, had even been classified as haiku prose, a kind of prose-poetry. The later sketch from life diaries, on the other hand, were closer to the poetic diaries (*uta-nikki*)[1] of the classical literature. While not every entry has a poem or poetic elements, enough do to make the comparison valid. Yet, the content is quite different from that of the classical poetic diaries, which usually were unified by a single narrative thread. Shiki's diaries have no plot; their unity is thematic, and resides in his character. In other words, his sketch from life prose culminated in a modern form of the poetic diary, modern (as were his haiku and tanka) in its emphasis on personality.

There are many ways in which poetry appears in the diaries. Sometimes it is as one or more haiku appended to an entry, sometimes as prose which is so compressed, intense and rhythmical that it seems close to free verse, sometimes as a series of tanka. There are long stretches where there is no poetry at all, it must be said, but still there is enough so that the poetry gives a special character to his diaries. One example is from the entry of April 28 in *A Drop of Ink*:

While lying on my back after dinner, I looked to my left; on top of the desk was a cluster of wisteria. Having taken up water very well, their flowers were in full bloom. Even as I murmured to myself, "How lovely, how perfectly lovely," the old days of poem-tales somehow came to mind and, strange though it was, I was moved to write some poems. I have become increasingly estranged from this discipline these days, and I took up my brush with some diffidence. . . .

kame ni sasu	wisteria
fuji no hanabusa	in the vase
mijikakereba	so short
tatami no ue ni	it doesn't touch
todokazarikeri	the floor
kame ni sasu	wisteria
fuji no hanabusa	in the vase—
hitofusa wa	one plume hangs down,
kasaneshi fumi no	brushing
ue ni taretari	a pile of books
fuji nami no	I see the wisteria
hana o shi mireba	that moves like waves
Nara no mikado	and longings rise
Kyō no mikado no	for Nara and Kyoto,
mukashi koishi mo	the ancient courtly days
fuji nami no	I see the wisteria
hana o shi mireba	that moves like waves
murasaki no	and think to take up
e no gu tori-ide	the purple paint
utsusan to omou	and sketch its likeness
fuji nami no	the purple of the wisteria
hana no murasaki	that moves like waves,
e ni kakeba	if made into a painting,

koki murasaki ni	would have to be
kakubekarikeri	a deep, deep purple
kame ni sasu	wisteria
fuji no hanabusa	in the vase
hana tarete	trails its plumes—
yamai no toko ni	at my sickbed, spring is
haru kuren to su	drawing to its close
[italics mine]	
kozo no haru	last spring
Kamedo ni fuji o	I saw wisteria
mishi koto o	at Kamedo—seeing
ima fuji o mite	the wisteria now
omoi idetsumo	brings it to mind
kurenai no	showing the way
botan no hana ni	to the crimson peonies,
sakidachite	the purple of
fuji no murasaki	the wisteria
saki-ide ni keri	has come into bloom
kono fuji wa	these wisteria
hayaku sakitari	have bloomed early . . .
Kameido no	the blossoming of
fuji sakamaku wa	those at Kameido will be
tōka mari nochi	more than ten days later
Yashiōri no	if soaked in
sake ni hitaseba	Yashiōri wine,
shioretaru	withered
fuji nami no hana	wisteria flowers
yomigaeri saku	will revive and bloom again

There are some rather overdone lines, but scribbling with my brush in the intervals left me by illness is a rare consolation these days. A strange spring night! (XI, 175–76)

The first poem says that the wisteria do not reach to the tatami where Shiki is lying. Its theme, discussed already in Chapter 4, is the gap between Shiki and the flower, human mortality and the ongoing life of nature. In the second poem, in contrast, the wisteria brushes a pile of books; here the point is that between the books and the wisteria there is no gap. The wisteria, as a flower popular in classical literature and possessing many literary associations, is connected to books, and so is Shiki, as a poet and a reader. The books thus become a neutral term connecting the poet and the flower and the connection between the human and natural worlds that was denied in the first poem is, indirectly, made.

In the third poem, one of the literary associations evoked by the wisteria is made explicit—"the ancient days of the world of Nara, the splendors of Kyoto," which are known through the poem-tales referred to in the prose foreword. With this poem, the focus of Shiki's attention changes from the flower physically present before him to its fellows in literature and art and his own personal associations with it.

As the wisteria moves out of nature and into culture, the sequence begins to move beyond the confines of the sick room and to acquire spatial and temporal extension. His thoughts having stretched, in the third poem, from the present wisteria backwards to "the ancient days," in the fourth poem Shiki thinks of reproducing the flower in a painting and, in the fifth poem, of how he would go about doing so.

This movement reproduces in poetry the process he had already reported in the prose foreword of the entry. There, while looking at the wisteria, "the old poem-tales somehow came to mind and, strange though it was, I was moved to write some poems." In the prose foreword, he was moved to write and here, in the poetic body, he is inspired (at least in thought) to paint.

The next thing the wisteria reminds him of, in the sixth poem, is spring; specifically, its end, a time which brought melancholy thoughts to Shiki, for he believed he would not live to see another spring.[2] The last three lines of the poem begin, respectively, with "flower," "illness," and "spring." In fact, when the poem is transcribed in the conventional five lines, the three words make a vertical ladder. Their proximity reinforces the association between the poet's imminent death (implied, as always in Shiki, by "illness," since the illness was fatal), spring, and the wisteria.

The wisteria as Shiki sees it has moved from being a part of nature in the first poem to being a part of culture ("the ancient days" of the poem-tale and painting) in the third through fifth poems, and now it becomes almost a part of Shiki. The gap asserted in the first poem between the natural and human worlds is closed. And as it is closed, a vision of the poet's own death looms in the background: in the flower's death he sees his own. This poem is the climax of the sequence.

The seventh poem, as though backing off from this unbearable identification, deals again with a perfectly normal, nonsymbolic, natural wisteria, seen at Kameido the previous spring. This poem is a bridge to the following three poems, as the second poem was to the third, fourth and fifth poems.

The last three poems are all ways of denying the finality of death: the eighth poem assumes the wisteria will die but affirms that they will be followed by the peonies, so that in a larger sense life will continue; the ninth poem speaks of the wisteria at Kameido (a variant spelling for Kamedo) that have not bloomed yet, so that more life is yet to come; the tenth poem asserts that even if the wisteria die, they can be resurrected. The afterword expresses a feeling of having been enchanted, in the literal sense, by the wisteria, though as always Shiki begins the passage straightforwardly.

The concern of the entry as a whole is death and mortality. In the tanka sequence, the wisteria are first seen as a symbol of life, opposite to Shiki. Through revery and art, the oppositeness is bridged. Then, when associated with spring's passing, they become identified with Shiki, a symbol of mortality. The identification is too painful and as if to deny death, the final three poems are concerned with new life springing up to replace old, and with resurrection.

The sequence has a unity of structure as well as theme. The first and sixth poems, the high points, are alike in that in both the wisteria remind Shiki of his own mortality; in the first poem, by their difference from him, and in the sixth by their similarity. As noted before, both are followed by a poem (two and seven) which functions as a bridge to the following three poems (three through five and eight through ten). As the concrete factuality of the first poem, an exemplary sketch from life, is followed by the more lyrical wishes and imaginings of the third through fifth poems, so the relative abstraction (spring's end) and lyricism of the sixth poem is followed by the flat statements of the last three poems.

Shiki's disciple Itō Sachio is usually credited with beginning the modern tanka sequence, but it can be seen from this example that the credit really belongs to Shiki, even if he did not explicitly state what he was doing. As a whole, the entry not only illustrates one of the ways in which Shiki combined poetry and prose, but also, as it traces the poet's interior monologue, depicts a complex stream of consciousness that, if developed further, could have become a chapter from a psychological novel. Critics of the haiku and the tanka had said that these forms were too brief to depict the complex thoughts of modern human beings, but here Shiki did just that, improving on a process begun as early as 1897, with the brief haiku sequence on the snow.

As there is poetry in the diaries which comes close to prose in its effect, so there are prose entries which come close to poetry in their compression, intensity and rhythmicality. One of these is the entry of June 6, from *A Drop of Ink,* where Shiki described himself intently listening to the sounds of the night around him when the pain kept him awake:

The nights are short now, but my illness keeps me from sleep. Gazing at the clock by the light of the oil lamp, I watch the hours slowly unfold.

1 A.M. A baby cries next door.

2 A.M. Far off I hear a rooster crow.

3 A.M. A solitary locomotive passes by.

4 A.M. The paper glued over a hole in the screen begins to grow light with the dawn; on the window ledge, the birds start to twitter in their crowded cage; then the sparrows; a little later, the crows.

5 A.M. Sound of a door being opened, then of water being drawn from a well; the world begins to fill with sound.

6 A.M. Shoes patter, rice bowls clink, hands clap, children are scolded. . . . Voices of good resound against voices of evil, swell to a chorus of hundreds, a thousand echoes answering, muffling, finally, the voice of my pain. (XI, 203)

The boundary between poetry and prose is a narrow one in any language. However, in Japanese it seems to me easier to cross than in

French and English, at least. Of the three possible ways to distinguish
verse from prose—rhyme, stress and syllable count—only the last is
available in Japanese. In the two most widely written traditional poetic
forms, the tanka and the haiku, the number of syllables in a line is
either seven or five; thus the tanka is 5/7/5/7/7 and the haiku
5/7/5. But alternating lines of five and seven syllables (5/7/5/7/5/
7/, etc.) are used to some extent in traditional prose as well, such as
the medieval military epics (the 13th century *Tale of the Heike,* for
example) and the Tokugawa period novels of Takizawa Bakin. True,
this is rhythmic prose, but it still shows the narrow border, on a formal
basis, between prose and poetry. Perhaps it is because of this that the
diction and subject matter suitable to different literary forms were
regulated very strictly.

The haiku, for example, traditionally used "season words" (*kigo*)
and "haiku words" (*haigon*) considered inappropriate to the tanka.
One of Shiki's innovations had been to use these words in the tanka,
thus helping to break down some of the distinction between the two
forms. In the tanka sequence on the wisteria, however, he used neither
season words nor haiku words, and the grammar was classical, as in
the traditional tanka. In a formal sense, the sequence obeys the
traditional conventions for poetry. The content, however, seemingly
factual and realistic, is far from the overt expression of emotion that
was traditionally considered poetic.

The prose entry of June 6 mixes characteristics of prose and poetry
in a somewhat different way. It insists, in the main, on the factual,
and describes it in the ordinary colloquial language of prose. The facts,
however, have an indefinable intensity that seems out of keeping with
the everyday quality of ordinary prose, and eventually explodes into
the phrase "voices of good resound against voices of evil, swell to a
chorus of hundreds, a thousand echoes answering, muffling, finally,
the voice of my pain."

Shiki's tenacious attachment to life as a human being, his elevation,
as a haiku theorist, of the role of observation to the level of a quasi-
mystical experience, and as a tanka poet, his creation of poems which
have the quality I referred to in Chapter 3 as "the consecration of the
everyday" are all related to the intensity, rhythmicality and compres-

sion of meaning that we feel in this piece of prose. It is certainly not poetry, but just as certainly it has some of the qualities of poetry.

Shiki's poetry is sometimes critized for being prosaic, too concerned with literal facts, not imaginative or emotional enough. But such criticism misses the point. In the haiku sequence on snow and the tanka sequence on wisteria, Shiki brilliantly exploited the narrow boundary between poetry and prose that his own language had given him. If such works can be accused of being prosaic poetry, they can also be praised as poetic prose.

Life and Literature: Shiki as the Diaries' Protagonist

Shiki dealt with his own death by creating literary works which had him for their protagonist and of which the theme was his own confrontation with mortality. In *A Drop of Ink* and *A Sixfoot Sickbed,* Shiki created a literary character, a persona, which was a refined and distilled version of the everyday Shiki we know from the private diary *Stray Notes While Lying On My Back* and some of the letters.

It might be argued that the private self of *Stray Notes* and the letters should be relegated to biography and the public self of *A Drop of Ink* and *A Sixfoot Sickbed* to literature, but in fact the two selves existed on a continuum, with the public self being a subtler, more refined version of the private, and, to some degree, created in the very act of writing. In this sense, the diaries are the stage on which Shiki finally achieved the equation of life and literature that followed from his sketch from life realism and which he asserted on a personal level as well. Just as Shiki's conscious aim as an artist practicing sketch from life realism was to create the illusion of an identity between art and reality, so his unconscious aim as a human being was to achieve an identity between his life and his literature. The motive for this was clear from his letter about Kyoshi of 1895 (see pages 23-24): the immortal self that existed on the printed page was to substitute for the all too mortal body that he was chained to in real life.[3]

From 1895, Shiki knew he would die young. For the seven remaining years of his life, much of the energy that was not devoted to his work as haiku editor for *Nippon* and as leader of his own literary movements, was taken up with meditation upon his own death. This was not due to a morbid fascination with the subject; it was forced upon him by the constant pain in which he lived.

In the end, writing was almost all he could do. As it came to be one of the last remaining physical activities he could perform voluntarily, more and more it became for him a metaphor for life itself. To write was to live, and when he could not lift the brush himself, he dictated to a friend. The title of *A Drop of Ink* shows how closely he identified his words with life, for the ink of the title was a metaphor for his life's blood.

From 1895 on, though he was uncertain when death would come, Shiki lived each day with its presence unbearably close. Time as he experienced it had qualities it does not have for most healthy people. First, it moved unbearably slowly and seemed extremely long, so that boredom was one of his chief torments. Second, and paradoxically, it seemed very short, moving swiftly and inexorably toward his own death. A sense of urgency, as expressed in the letter of 1895 about Kyoshi, coexisted with a sense of enormous tedium. Thirdly, time had no firmly imaginable future, for he felt he could not plan for more than a few hours ahead. There was only a past and a present. Death, though he knew it would come, was a darkness, unimaginable; he did not believe in an afterlife. These are the qualities time has when experienced in the midst of great anxiety over a portending and dreaded, but in some ways desired, event.

Shiki's anxiety over death was intimately bound up with his pain. An increase in physical pain, which signified the further deterioration of his body, always brought in its train depression, anxiety, and ultimately great mental agitation. These emotions then increased the pain itself.

To his anxiety and his pain, the twin prisons in which he lived, Shiki considered a limited number of solutions—to dream or go mad, to destroy himself, or to beguile the time by activity. Although he expressed the wish to go mad, he was too incurably rational to do so. He seems, however, to have often had dreams in which he walked and even flew in painless freedom, or else found a blissful death. In the entry of April 24 from *A Drop of Ink*, he wrote,

Last night I had a dream. I had come to a place where many animals were playing. One of them was rolling about in such agony that I was certain it was about to die. A gentle rabbit went up to the tormented beast and offered its paw. The animal at once took the rabbit's paw in both of its own and pressed it to its lips. Just as it joyfully started to kiss the paw, its suffering ended and it died as though falling into a blissful sleep. The rabbit then did the same for another animal who was raving in the throes of death; and that animal also yielded to death as if to a pleasant sleep. I have woken from my dream but I shall never forget that rabbit. (XI, 170–71)

In two memorable passages, Shiki spoke of a different sort of dream as one means of escape. In *A Drop of Ink* for May 15, 1901, he wrote:

I hate the month of May. Feeling it in the air the last few days has made me unbearably depressed. I can't collect my thoughts at all.

Even now, though, I stroll about quite happily in my dreams. But when I have to jump over things, I always bend my head. . . .

When my body is pressed down by pain, I have no defense but to wish I could float gently through the sky, touching nothing—as though the specific gravity of air and man were the same. . . .

Last year at this time, I could go as far as the next room by crawling. This year it's difficult just to turn in my bed. Next year at this time I shall probably be unable to move. (XI, 189)

In *A Sixfoot Sickbed* for August 10, 1902, he contrasted the freedom he enjoyed in dreams with the suffering he endured while awake:

I dreamt that plum, cherry and peach trees had blossomed all at once and I walked about here and there on a lovely hillside and said to someone, "There is no greater happiness than this." It was while I slept, but still, how could I have such a dream when my health these days is such that I am never free from pain? (XI, 345)

And yet, Shiki was unable to take the one step that would have freed him forever from pain. The climactic entry of his private journal *Stray Notes While Lying On My Back* (October 13, 1901) made this clear. After pages and pages devoted to the interminable boredom of his bedridden existence, he described a day when no visitors came and his exasperation reached a peak. His mother, unable to distract him, could only reply with the stock phrase, "It can't be helped" (*Shikata ga nai*). Finally, he sent her out with a telegram addressed to his haiku disciple Sakamoto Shihōda bearing the single word, "Come." While she was gone, Shiki contemplated suicide. All that prevented him from carrying out the impulse was his physical inability to make a clean job of it and thus the knowledge that it would be necessary to suffer still more on the way to death:

Alone in the quiet house, still lying on my left side, I saw . . . a blunt penknife about two inches long and an eyeleteer of the same size on the inkstone box. . . . The suicide mania, which sometimes arises even without such inspiration, came on me like a fury. In fact, the idea had passed through my mind already, while writing the telegram. But I thought, "I won't be able to kill myself with that blunt penknife or the eyeleteer. I know there's a razor in the next room. If only I had that razor, I could slit my throat. Unfortunately, I can't even crawl now. It's not that I couldn't cut my windpipe with this penknife, if I had to. And I'm sure I'd die if I punctured my chest with the eyeleteer. But I don't want my suffering to be prolonged. I wonder if I would die instantaneously if I made three or four holes. . . ." So my thoughts went.

But in the end, fear won out, and I couldn't bring myself to do it. It is not death I fear, but suffering. I can't bear the pain of my illness as it is. I am afraid I would fail to die as well. . . . I was seized with terror today when I looked at the penknife. I stared at it, thinking, "I'll just hold it in my hand and look at it." Finally, about to pick it up, I thought, "This is it, this is it!", ready to go all the way. "I'll take it!" "No, I won't"—the two thoughts battled in my mind. In the midst of them, I broke into sobs. . . . Blood rushed to my head, and I couldn't open my eyes. Unable to open my eyes, I couldn't read the paper, and so I could not help thinking. Then I remembered death would come soon. Feeling it near, I wanted only to enjoy myself until it came, and so I conceived a craving for a delicious meal. But for that, I needed money—and so I even thought of selling my books—oh no, no! how could I sell my books! At that point, my thoughts became hopelessly entangled and the rush of blood to my head became a fury. (XI, 466–67)

In the passage above, particularly the last part (from "Blood rushed to my head"), the function of activity in enabling Shiki to forget his anxiety over death is apparent, and so is the near-identity of his boredom and his anxiety. His boredom was not a fin-de-siècle world-weariness, but an intense desperation. Yet, unable to bring himself to commit suicide, he had to beguile the time by activity—by writing, sketching, reading, eating—the only volitional activities he was still capable of, although he could not perform even these all the time.

The three diaries of 1901 and 1902 represent part of Shiki's efforts to distract himself by activity. The impulse to write and publish *A Drop of Ink,* in particular, was rooted in Shiki's need to reaffirm his existence daily as he watched the daily, visible wasting away of his body. In the January 24 entry of this journal, he wrote that he meant it only as a diversion for himself from the tedium of illness and did not expect anyone else to take it seriously. Yet, there is no doubt that he himself took it very seriously, if not as literature then as an expression of his life, for he begged shamelessly to have it published serially in *Nippon,* even though the editors were far from enthusiastic.

Shortly before the journal began to appear in *Nippon,* Shiki wrote the following letter to his close friend and haiku disciple Samukawa Sokotsu, a member of *Nippon*'s editorial board:

The pain in my side had made it impossible for me to write recently. I was in a terrible state of depression and boredom. But suddenly the idea came to me of writing a short essay (between one and twenty lines) for the newspaper every day, and calling it *A Drop of Ink,* and the evening before last I sent off the first installment. Last night I sent off another. Then, thinking it would appear this morning, I rushed to open the newspaper only to find that it wasn't there. Filled with disgust and despair, all desire to read anything, even the newspaper, left me.

But as I looked over the layout, I noticed that the newspaper was filled to the brim with long articles. I suppose there was no room left for *A Drop of Ink.* However, I'm not choosy. The margins would be fine. In fact, they might be even better. I could use two margins every day and play about at marginal literature. You wouldn't lend me two margins by any chance, would you? If I had the money, it would be fun to run my writing as advertisements. I'd buy some space every day and publish myself in the classifieds. Wouldn't that be amusing?

I have few pleasures in my illness. When I am disappointed, there is nothing to help me forget. A man with strong legs can complain without a

second thought, "I've had all I can take. I'm going off somewhere!" But a
man who can't walk can't even do that. I have no choice. As you once begged
of me, I beg of you. (XIX, 604–605)

At the time Shiki wrote this letter, he was still editor of the haiku
column of *Nippon* (a position he retained until July 1901, when illness
forced him to pass on his position to Hekigotō). Sokotsu was one of
his closest friends. The two had grown up together in Matsuyama, and
Shiki had not only helped Sokotsu to take his first steps in haiku, but
had secured for him his job at *Nippon*. Shiki himself was a protégé of
Kuga Katsunan, the editor-in-chief of *Nippon*. There could have been
little doubt in Shiki's mind that the newspaper would, eventually,
publish anything of his he asked. He had no need to "beg" his disciple
to publish his work, and he did not: he begged him to publish his
work *every day*.

Shiki's ever present sense of death made him need a daily reminder
that he was alive. If words were life to him (as his letter of 1895
about Kyoshi indicated) then his published diary must have been
tangible proof to him of his own survival. In that sense, the "short
pieces" of *A Drop of Ink* were Shiki's own life transfigured into
words, expressions of an effort to recreate himself in words as his body
literally decayed before his eyes. They were his way, as well, of
clinging tenaciously to this world.

An attachment to life provided the basic impulse for all three
diaries. This attachment is expressed most concretely in the private
diary *Stray Notes,* which stresses the physical aspect of his life almost
to the point of tedium. The typical entry begins with a comment on
how he slept, a listing of all food eaten that day, with exact quantities,
the number of bowel movements he had, the weather, the events in
his garden (what birds came, what flowers were in bloom), and the
general state of his illness. Some entries add nothing more. Others, if
he felt well enough, note the day's social events, such as the names of
visitors and the presents, if any, they brought. Rather frequently the
physical concerns are expressed in or provide the background for
poems. There are a few very long entries—one in which he vents his
rage against his sister Ritsu and another in which he vents it against
Nakae Chōmin,[4] the author of *Ichinen Yūhan* [A Year and A Half);

and a third, in which he describes a brush with suicide, already quoted. Aside from these three expressions of pent-up emotion, most of the entries are short.

In *Stray Notes,* which Shiki did not intend anyone else to see, he made little effort to achieve literary interest. Almost all entries are written in a mixture of katakana and kanji, and the work as a whole gives the impression of the barest sort of diary. Yet it has tremendous fascination. It is liberally sprinkled with poems and drawings, as though these were so natural to Shiki that they poured from his pen even when he was at his most literal. The contrast between the completely physical and raw concerns of most of the prose and the more refined emotions expressed in the bulk of the poetry is very striking, creating a strange mixture of a grossly material perception of experience with a refined distillation of it in the form of art. I doubt that there has been anything like it in Japanese literature before or since.

The tenacious grasp on life that Shiki expressed through writing the diaries was accompanied by a paradoxical desire to be rid of it; living itself had become an agony. The extreme of this desire was reached in the suicidal thoughts already quoted from *Stray Notes.* But other reactions indicate that his inner resources were deeper than the account from *Stray Notes* suggests and also help one understand how he was able to carry on his literary activities for so long. In *A Sixfoot Sickbed* for June 2, 1902, he wrote,

> Until now I had mistaken the "Enlightenment" of Zen: I was wrong to think it meant being able to die serenely under any conditions. It means being able to live serenely under any conditions. (XI, 261)

In two of the most moving entries of *Stray Notes,* Shiki described himself as he watched his body decay. On October 2, 1901, he wrote:

> For a few days, the lower left side of my abdomen (a pelvic bone?) has been more painful than usual, so when the diaper was changed I took a look. It had become completely black, as though decayed. I am sure another fistula will open. I don't care what happens to a body I've long since given up on; still, it doesn't make me feel very good to think another fistula may develop.

With this on my mind, I ate lunch, but it didn't taste as good as usual, and while eating my eyes filled with tears from time to time. (XI, 456)

On March 10, 1902, in the first entry made since October 29 of the previous year, he wrote:

Today I was surprised when I looked at the fistula on my stomach for the first time. I had thought it would be small, but it is a hollow. I became sad and wept. (XI, 486)

Pain was as great a factor in Shiki's despair as boredom and was at least partly responsible for his ambivalence toward life. Sometimes he wished to die as an escape from his suffering; but always, or almost always, his attachment to life conflicted with this. This ambivalence, treated so directly in *Stray Notes*, was conveyed more subtly and humorously in *A Drop of Ink* and *A Sixfoot Sickbed*, probably because both of the latter were intended for publication. (In the May 11 entry of *A Drop of Ink* Shiki wrote, "Put some poison beside my bed. Would I take it or not?"; this was not published in *Nippon*.) In *A Drop of Ink* especially, Shiki treated his conflict with humor and irony, transmuting the theme of ambivalence into a kind of game in which he sought out death only to engage it in shadow-boxing, playing with it, teasing it, asking it to come take him, then suddenly getting cold feet. For example, in the entry of April 9 he addressed a letter to the Four Elements:

1902

Earth, Water, Fire, Wind & Co.:
   Re: One Human Being.
         I return same. However, please accord it special
   dispensation to return to this world from time to time as
   a spirit.

Yours truly,
Masaoka Shiki (XI, 159)

There is also the marvelous fantasy of his visit to Enma, lord of the underworld, in the entry for May 21 from the same diary:

I am standing at the foot of a table presided over by Enma, Lord of the Dead.

"I wish to make a request," I say.

"What is it?" Enma bellows in reply.

Then I politely make my appeal, explaining that I am Masaoka Shiki, an invalid of Negishi. I tell him that I am there to ascertain why no one from his bureau has come to fetch me yet, even though I am ready and waiting to be taken away, and that I wish to know when I can expect someone to come. At once, Lord Enma obligingly looks in his register for 1901, but cannot find my name. He gets a little flustered as he searches, and great beads of sweat roll down his face, but finally he discovers my name, crossed out, in the register for May 1897.[5] The notation says that Blue Demon Number Five had gone to fetch me, so he summons Blue Demon Number Five and inquires into the matter. The demon replies,

"I went to get him, but the streets of Negishi twist and turn so much that I couldn't find the house and finally turned back."

Red Demon Number Eleven, who had gone to fetch me the second time, is summoned and interrogated. He answers,

"Oh, yes, I went. But when I reached the sign saying 'Nightingale Lane,' I saw the street was too narrow for the Cart of Fire[6] to pass through, so I came back."

Lord Enma looks very upset when he hears this, but Lord Jizō,[7] who is next to him, says,

"In view of the circumstances, give him another ten years of life, as a favor to me."

Frantically, I say,

"What a terrible idea! No one would mind another ten years of life if he were healthy, but if I am to pass my time in the kind of pain I'm enduring now, I want to be taken away as soon as possible. I couldn't stand another year of this torture!"

Suddenly Lord Enma seems to take pity on me.

"If that's how you feel, I'll come for you tonight!"

I am a bit taken aback.

"Tonight is too soon."

"How about tomorrow evening?"

"Don't torment me so cruelly! I want to be taken by surprise."

Lord Enma smiles sardonically.

"Very well, then, I'll do it without warning. You should realize, however, that your surprise might come tonight."

"Lord Enma, I don't enjoy being threatened." (This à la Kikugorō).[8]
Lord Enma guffaws,
"This guy really has a mind of his own!" (This à la Sadanji). Wooden
clappers.
Curtain. (XI, 193–95)

One basic, single-minded wish underlay Shiki's ambivalence: to be
released from suffering. It was a hopeless wish; no human being could
do more than distract him from it for a time. His most intense physical
experience, that of pain, was one that no other human being could
share, though to him it was so overwhelmingly real that it sometimes
blotted out consciousness of all else. In *A Sixfoot Sickbed* for May 28,
1902, he wrote that his pain was "indescribable" and only someone
who had died once or was on the verge of death could understand
what he experienced. Other people on their deathbeds, he went on,
had berated those nearby (he gave some historical examples), so he
felt he was not alone in his rebukes to his family. One case in
particular interested him. Shiki had never met this sick man, Bujian
(his real name and other identification are unknown), but the two had
felt a mutual sympathy because they suffered from the same disease
and had even carried on a correspondence until Bujian's death late in
the spring of 1901.

After Bujian's death, some members of his family visited Shiki and
he was struck by the similarity between Bujian's conduct as an invalid,
as reported by these relatives, and his own, as he observed it in
himself. The parallels were: not letting his nurses (that is, his mother
and sister) leave his bedside for even a moment, being angry when his
demands were not fulfilled before he had even finished expressing
them, finding it difficult to breathe in the presence of a large person,
showing intense likes and dislikes about people, and being subject to
extremes of happiness and depression. They were alike, he went on,
even in such details as feeling pain when the coverlet was hard, but
feeling buried and equally in pain if it were soft. They both overate.
And if visitors said they did not look as thin as feared, both would
furiously stick out their match-stick thin legs and demand bitterly,
"How about these?" (XI, 256).

In addition to such disciples as Hekigotō, Sokotsu, and perhaps Kyoshi, as well as his friend Fusetsu and neighbor and editor Katsunan, Bujian was one of the few human beings who gave Shiki any solace.

Shiki's relations with his mother and sister seem to have been difficult even though they nursed him devotedly after he became an invalid. The vignette of his mother in the episode from *Stray Notes* quoted already makes her sound a rather ineffectual person. Elsewhere in the diary, he claimed that both she and his sister were completely lacking in the imaginative resources necessary to cheer an invalid like himself (I can not resist adding that they were probably too busy simply accomplishing the basic tasks of life—cleaning, laundry, cooking, and attending to Shiki's medical needs, as well as waiting on the guests who came to call—to have much time to spare for imagination).

Shiki's particular wrath was reserved for his sister Ritsu, who became the subject of one of the most extraordinary series of entries in *Stray Notes*. On September 20, he wrote, the stiff simplicity of the katakana in which he set it down emphasizing the intensity of his fury:

Ritsu is a literal-minded woman. She is like an unfeeling tree or stone. She will nurse an invalid dutifully but can not comfort him emotionally. She will do anything the invalid orders, but is incapable of taking a hint. For example, the invalid may repeatedly call out, "Some dumplings would taste good right now!", but even though she hears him, nothing sinks in. When a sick man says such a thing, any compassionate person would immediately go out and buy him some dumplings. Ritsu alone would never think of that. Therefore, if I want to eat some dumplings, I must give her an explicit command, "Go buy me some dumplings." She never opposes such a command. Her literal-mindedness is infuriating. She shows an equal lack of feeling for everyone except for the canary, for whom she seems to have true compassion. She can stay motionless in front of the canary's cage for an hour or two at a time, simply gazing. But she hates to stay by the invalid's side. I tried explaining to her what compassion means, but a person without compassion can hardly be expected to understand it, and my efforts were of no use. It's depressing, but I must resign myself to it. (XI, 428)

The next day he wrote,

Ritsu is obstinate. She is indifferent to people. She is especially 'shy' [the English word is used] with men. She is completely unsuited to be a wife. That is why she ended up as her brother's nurse. If I hadn't had her after I became sick, how would I have gotten along until now? I could not have employed a professional nurse for any length of time, and even if I could, no nurse would be better than Ritsu, or able to do as much as she does. Ritsu is a combination of nurse, housemaid, housekeeper, and secretary. It is true that she does not take perfect care of my books and that she is not an ideal copyist for my manuscripts, but at least she does both, and she doesn't cost even one-tenth the salary a professional nurse would demand. She is satisfied with just one dish, whether vegetable or pickles or anything else doesn't matter—with that, her meal is complete. It never seems to occur to her to buy meat or fish for herself. If she were away for even a day, the household would not only stop in its tracks but I would be almost unable to go on living. That is why I need not worry no matter how serious my illness becomes. I only pray that she does not fall ill. As long as she remains healthy, all will be well. If anything happened to her, the whole household would flounder. So I always hope that rather than her falling ill, I will die. Twice she has married and twice returned. Was she a failure as a wife because she was obscurely fated to become her brother's nurse? The complexities of fortune and misfortune are not within the realm of man's knowledge.

aki no hae	autumn fly—
hae tataki mina	all the fly swatters
yaburetari	are broken[9]

byōshitsu ya	sickroom—
mado atataka ni	on the warm window
aki no hae	an autumn fly

"May everything in the universe become a Buddha":

hechima sae	hey!—even snake gourds
hotoke ni naru zo	become Buddhas—
okururu na	don't get caught behind![10]

jōbutsu ya	Buddha-death:
yūgao no kao	the moonflower's face,
hechima no he	the snake gourd's fart[11]

She is a touchy person. She is stubborn. She is awkward. She hates to ask questions. She is terribly clumsy with her hands. Once something is decided, she cannot change. Her faults are infinite. She has angered me so much that at times I have wanted to kill her. However, I cherish her all the more deeply because she is, in fact, a psychological cripple. I worry that if she ever had to make her way alone in the world, she would suffer greatly from her faults, and so I am always trying to reform her quick temper. I wonder if she will remember my admonitions at all when she has lost me.

As my condition becomes more severe and the pain increases, I am constantly scolding people when things don't go as I wish. My family is afraid to come near me. I have no one who understands the true meaning of nursing. (XI, 430–32)

Another object of Shiki's wrath was Nakae Chōmin. Shiki referred to Chōmin's book *A Year and a Half* in several passages throughout his works, but nowhere more entertainingly and poignantly than in *Stray Notes* for October 25, 1901.

An introductory note is in order: Chōmin, informed by his doctor that he had a year and a half to live, had immediately written a book of philosophical reflections inspired by his plight and it had become a best-seller. Shiki, by contrast, had encountered difficulties publishing the diaries of his illness even in serial form in a newspaper; and although they were widely read, they were by no means as widely discussed or as popular as Chōmin's work. Unlike Chōmin, moreover, Shiki had derived little profit from his publications and had to live in part on the charity of his friends.

In the entry in question, Shiki dismissed *A Year and a Half* as shallow and ascribed its popularity to the sympathy readers felt for someone on the verge of death. Recently, he went on, someone (unconnected to Chōmin) had written the newspaper *Niroku Shimpō* to announce his own intention of killing himself. This letter attracted such wide attention that not only did the writer decide to continue living, but he received three hundred yen (the equivalent of several thousand dollars today) worth of presents. Someone had even offered to open a tobacco shop for him. "[He and] *A Year and a Half* make a well-matched couple," Shiki wrote bitterly, and went on,

Realizing how little time I have left in which to eat, I am filled with the desire to eat delicious food while I can. But since I cannot expect an elaborate meal (the kind one might order, for example, from a restaurant) from my mother or sister, I yearn for some spending money of my own. I strain my mind for ideas, but the only solution I can think of is to sell my books. But I have none suitable for sale. At one point, I thought of selling some books I have which are bound Western-style and some other single volumes, but all were stamped with the Otter's Study seal from my student days, and I would have been ashamed to have anyone see them. After thinking over various plans, I decided in the end to borrow twenty yen from Kyoshi. I've already received eleven yen in cash. Even though we call it a loan, I have no expectation of returning it. I hope someone will return it for me after I die. I ought to write a promissory note saying that if no one does, Kyoshi is free to take away the furniture, household goods, books, and anything else in my house.

Managing to lay my hands on twenty yen (as described above), even though I am on the verge of death, seems like a pretty good performance for me, though it can't compare to *A Year and a Half* or the letter writer who earned himself a tobacco shop. But in any case to put one's life up for sale is worth nothing but contempt.

> byōshō no
> saifu mo aki no
> nishiki kana

> the wallet
> by the bed is my
> autumn brocade[12]

> kurimeshi ya
> byōnin nagara
> ōkurai

> chestnut rice—
> though a sick man,
> still a glutton

> kaburitsuku
> jukushi ya hige o
> yogoshikeri

> I sink my teeth
> into a ripe persimmon—
> it dribbles down my beard

> odoroku ya
> yūgao ochishi
> yowa no oto

> surprise!
> a moonflower fell—
> midnight sound (XI, 479)

Shiki was estranged from the world and was acutely aware that he was estranged. The very first entry of *A Sixfoot Sickbed* created the image of Shiki as a man unwillingly set apart from all other human beings:

A sixfoot sickbed—this is my world. And yet, it is too large for me. I manage to reach out my hand and touch the tatami, but I cannot stretch my legs outside the coverlet and lie at ease. At the worst times, I cannot move at all without suffering extreme pain. Pain, anguish, wailing, medicine to numb me—the vanity of coveting a bit of comfort, of seeking a path that turns off the highway to death! And yet, as long as I am alive, there are things I want to say. My daily reading matter is confined to newspapers and magazines, but the pain often keeps me from reading even those. Yet, when I do read, I sometimes grow angry or disgusted; or, rarely, I forget the pain of my illness in an indefinable joy. I say by way of introduction that such are feelings of an invalid who has lain in bed every day for six years apart from the world. (XI, 231)

Shiki's sense of alienation from those more fortunate than himself might have turned him into a querulous, self-pitying invalid interested in no one but himself. Yet even in *Stray Notes,* which is so centered on Shiki's physical condition that one comes to feel immersed in Shiki's body and its ingestions, digestions, and eliminations, the awareness of beauty is never completely lost and there is a poem, sketch, or painting on virtually every page.

No matter how petty and self-absorbed Shiki became, his love of beauty tied him to the world. Perhaps the most moving example is the brief entry of April 15 in *A Drop of Ink,* a summation of Shiki's relation to the world:

There is a glass bowl with ten goldfish in it on my desk. I am gazing at it from my bed, as the pain assaults me. I feel the pain and see the beauty. (XI, 164)

Shiki's creativity in the diaries was an expression of his love of beauty as well as of his desire to transmute his life into words. Five of his greatest tanka sequences are in *A Drop of Ink*; they were written in a creative spurt of two weeks from April 28 through May 11, 1901, and include the sequence already discussed on the wisteria as well as the following (of which the first and the sixth were discussed in Chapter 3).

May 4

        Forcing myself to take up the brush—
Saogami no   ah, sad to part
wakare kanashi mo   from Lady Sao—
kon haru ni   in the spring to come
futatabi awan   it will not be me
ware naranaku ni   who meets her again

ichihatsu no   the wall iris
hana saki-idete   opens its buds:
wagame ni wa   before my eyes
kotoshi bakari no   the last spring
haru yukan to su   begins to fade

yamu ware wo   as if to cheer me
nagusame gao ni   on my bed of pain
hirakitaru   the peony spreads
botan no hana wo   its petals wide, and
mireba kanashi mo   seeing this I grieve

yo no naka wa   thinking how soon
tsunenaki mono to   all in this world passes
waga mezuru   I loved
yamabuki no hana   the yellow roses
chirinikeru kamo   that now have scattered

wakareyuku   in memory of
haru no katami to   the spring now passing
fujinami no   I drew
hana no nagafusa   the long clusters of wisteria
e ni kakeru kamo   that move like waves

yūgao no   I dream of making
tana tsukuran to   a trellis for moon-flowers
omoedomo   to climb
aki machigatenu   but oh my life that will not
waga inochi kamo   bear the wait till autumn!

kurenai no   the crimson roses
ubara fufuminu   have come into bud—

waga yamai	omen of the time
iyamasarubeki	when my illness
toki no shirushi ni	will grow worse

Satsuma geta	I remember plucking
ashi ni torihaki	buds of bush clover
tsue tsukite	long ago with
hagi no me tsumishi	Satsuma geta on my feet and
mukashi omōyu	a walking stick in my hand

wakamatsu no	the green of the young
medachi no midori	pine seedlings . . .
nagaki hi wo	as the long day
yūkata makete	succumbs to night
netsu idenikeri	my fever rises

itatsuki no	I do not know the day
iyuru hi shirani	my pain will end yet
saniwabe ni	in the little garden
akikusabana no	I had them plant
tane o makashimu	seeds of autumn flowers

People will only think me sentimental. (XI, 179–80)

While the creative efflorescence of *A Drop of Ink* had come in tanka, that of *A Sixfoot Sickbed* came through painting. In the last months of his life, Shiki became more devoted than ever to making watercolor sketches from life (*shasei*) of plants, flowers, fruit, and vegetables. He kept one notebook for plants and flowers and another for fruits and vegetables; some of the sketches were published in *A Sixfoot Sickbed* as it was serialized in *Nippon*. On August 6, 1902, somewhat over a month before his death, he wrote:

These days my greatest pleasure is to sketch from life after taking morphine [emphasis in original]. Today it was rainy as usual and my head was so groggy I couldn't bear it. I took some morphine in the morning and sketched the Ezo chrysanthemum from life. The first try was a terrible failure, but the next one was fairly successful and I was delighted. (XI, 343)

On August 7, he wrote simply,

> I had a flowering branch put beside my pillow. As I faithfully sketch it, I
> feel I am gradually coming to understand the secret of creation. (XI, 344)

In *A Sixfoot Sickbed,* Shiki became able, perhaps thanks to
morphine, to forget his pain at intervals and achieve a kind of quiet
joy. Whether his painting had actually improved I cannot say, but his
response to beauty seems to have become more intense as he became
closer to death. Paradoxically, the closer he came to the final
dissolution, the more he came to feel he understood the secret of
creation. On August 9, he wrote,

> When I mix various colors as I paint flowers, yet still do not achieve the
> effect I want, I try yet another color. Red can have different effects depending
> on the shading. One of the joys of sketching from life lies in pondering how
> to obtain a slightly darker red or a rather more yellowish one. When the
> gods first dyed the flowers did they too lose themselves in musings like this?
> (XI, 344)

In *A Drop of Ink,* Shiki had written, "I feel the pain and see the
beauty." This ability to hold two opposites in suspension, preserving
both yet yielding to neither, has already been described in the poetry,
and it characterized Shiki himself as well, for he tended both to
perceive and to describe in dualities.

A Drop of Ink, for example, abounds in discussions of dualities:
city life versus country life, the old calendar versus the new, Japan
versus the West, good poetry versus bad, subjectivity versus objectivity,
as well as the already mentioned oppositions of pain and beauty,
sickness and health, the desire to live and the desire to die.

Some of the contrasts are playful, as in the entry for February 11:

> When I woke up that morning and looked outside, the earth was mantled
> in white. The snow was no longer falling, but the sky was still dark with
> clouds. I rushed over to the athletic field of my high school. The early arrivals
> were milling about in groups according to their grades and classes. Everyone
> was waving banners and flags with phrases like "Celebration of the
> Promulgation of the Constitution" and "Banzai for the Empire" written on

them. One stood out from all the rest: a red and white banner, fluttering
bravely in the piercing wind. We watched the Imperial carriage pass Nijū-
bashi and shouted "Banzai!" three times. Afterwards, I decided to go to a
celebratory party at a friend's house in Shiba instead of rejoining the school
parade. On the way there, I picked up a magazine. It was the first issue of
Nippon, with a copy of the Constitution as a supplement, and a picture of the
Three Imperial Treasures on the cover—childish, one might say of me now,
but I found it of great interest. Then I went on to the party. But before I had
had enough of the food booths, street dances and entertainments, it grew
dark. I went home, making my way over the frozen mud—February 11,
twelve years ago. Twelve years is quite a long time. Since then, *Nippon* has
reached the pinnacle of health, and I have become a helpless cripple. But will
the Constitution that was born then ever walk on firm legs? (XI, 106)

After recounting how he spent the day that the first issue of *Nippon*
appeared and the Constitution was promulgated, in the last sentence
he contrasts his own progress since then with the newspaper's—
"*Nippon* has reached the pinnacle of health, and I have become a
helpless cripple"—and wonders if the Constitution will ever learn to
walk.

In the entry for March 7, he relates at length how the birds outside
his window bathe, then notes at the end that *he* has not been able to
bathe for five years. The sudden shift of viewpoint here, as in the
entry for February 11, gives a flourish and vivacity to all that comes
before:

After I became sick, someone borrowed a large wire birdcage for me to
take my mind off being confined to bed. I had it placed in front of the
window with ten birds inside. I enjoy watching them from my sickbed, for
they have a funny way of rushing down to bathe when the water in their
basin is changed. Before one can even take one's hand off the water basin and
out of the cage, the finches fly down, ahead of any of the others. They are the
best bathers, too, splashing away so energetically that half the water is gone
in a minute. Then the other birds have to take turns bathing in what little
water is left. I doubt whether the two black-headed mannikins consciously
decided to change matters, but lately they fly down just as the finches are
about to hop in, then chase them away and bathe themselves side by side.
After them come the Jakarta sparrows and then the zebra finches and the
canaries. Finally the basin's edge is thronged with birds arranged in order of

arrival. Each flies up to the perch as it finishes bathing and flaps its wings furiously. They look so happy. Now that I think of it, it must be about five years since I could take a bath. (XI, 130–31)

The mood of the two public diaries, even when Shiki is describing emotions that were truly pitiful, is always informed by this quality of playfulness. Job had the majestic Jehovah to rail against in his misery; Shiki, whose misfortunes were nearly as great and certainly as undeserved, provided himself with comic figures like the lord of the dead who cannot keep his record books straight and unseen cosmic forces who organized themselves into a business firm.

But even at his most playful, Shiki employed his special ability to speak of two opposing ideas in one breath. When the one was the surface meaning of a statement and the other its true meaning, the result could be biting sarcasm. When they were contradictory feelings within himself, he could create a mood of light-hearted irony. And when they were his own isolation and the world's plenitude of life and beauty, as in the entries of May 15 and June 6 from *A Drop of Ink,* he could evoke an emotion moving beyond words.

Taken as a whole, the diaries give a full picture of Shiki's physical and mental state during the last two years of his life. The contents are amazingly varied, ranging from haiku, tanka and Chinese poetry, to personal reminiscences, literary and art criticism, still-life watercolor sketches, lists of presents received, ethnological notes, tormented outpourings of his pain and frustration, minor essays on his daily life, and humorous reflections on the world outside his sickroom as mediated by the newspapers and magazines of the day. Yet the premise and central theme of each was his physical deterioration. Running like a stream through the diaries, sometimes disappearing while poetic or intellectual interests take the lead, then abruptly surfacing for a time only to go underground again, were the anger, frustration, despair, and self-pity of a man who had to wait helplessly for death. Even the reader who has never suffered as Shiki did can identify with the feelings Shiki expressed: his experience was but an extreme form of the universal confrontation with suffering and death. Anyone who has ever had the barest intimation of this confrontation will be caught by the truth of the diaries and find it hard to turn away from Shiki's voice as it speaks so clearly across the barriers of language, culture, and time.

Summary

The inner conflicts precipitated by adherence to contradictory value systems can be either paralyzing or stimulating, depending on the individual. In Shiki's case the conflict between the traditional Confucian contempt for literature and the nascent respect for it among Japanese intellectuals in the early Meiji period colored his adolescence and early adulthood. A sense that literature, especially the haiku, was not worthy of an intellectual's serious attention at first prevented him from making the commitment that would have been natural for one of his aptitude and leanings; but in the end, he did. The route by which he finally achieved a sense that the haiku could be justifiable in Confucian terms is described in earlier chapters. Suffice it to say here that the solution consisted of applying Confucian *gakumon* ("scholarship") to the haiku and at the same time insisting on the identity of the haiku as part of that new cultural category spawned by the Meiji period, *bungaku* ("serious literature").

Once Shiki had found his solution and begun to expound it in the form of haiku criticism and poems, the magnetism of his intellect and personality swept many of the brightest young men of his generation along in his path. Had his value conflict precipitated a personal disintegration, his life might have ended in suicide or some other less extreme form of psychological paralysis. But fortunately Shiki was able to summon up, instead, a creative response, which not only changed him but also resulted in the revitalization of the haiku in the Meiji period and the determination of its tendencies down to the present day.

In his last years, another fact began to dominate Shiki's life, namely his illness. Tuberculosis was an even more formidable threat to the integrity of the personality than the earlier conflict of values. On a physical level, it meant, eventually, unendurable pain. On the emotional level, because of the longing for death as a release from pain, it created a profound ambivalence between the wish to live and the wish to die. At times this ambivalence made him hysterical, even suicidal; at other times he viewed it with humor or ironic detachment. And at still other times he was able to transcend it, expressing a sense of the simultaneous and harmonious coexistence of life and death, being and nonbeing. It is this transcendent state that characterizes the most moving poems and prose of his last years, especially the poems discussed in the third part of Chapter 3 and the diaries dealt with in Chapter 5.

As with his earlier dilemma, the solution to Shiki's conflicting attractions to life and death was a creative one whose terms went beyond the merely personal. In fact, if his earlier reintegration of forces at war within the self had affected many of his generation, this later one had the potential to affect anyone in the world, for it had universal literary, and human, meaning. Shiki expressed the simultaneous existence of life and death as he experienced it himself, but in speaking of himself he also spoke of more. His own fatal illness became a shorthand for human mortality, the "fatal illness" that afflicts us all.

Notes and References

Preface

1. Readers interested in haiku after Shiki are referred to Furuta Soichi, *Cape Jasmine and Pomegranates: the free-meter haiku of Ippekiro* (New York: Grossman Publishers, 1974). Ueda Makoto, *Modern Japanese Haiku: An Anthology* (Toronto, Canada: University of Toronto Press, 1975).

2. Earl Miner, *Japanese Poetic Diaries* (Berkeley and Los Angeles, 1969), was the first to examine the Japanese poetic diary as a form bridging traditional and modern literature.

3. In the October 1978 issue of *Haiku to Essei,* Hirai Terutoshi argued that Shiki was not exclusively a realistic poet but that many of his poems were based on imagination. In the same issue, Miyazaki Toshihide asserted that Shiki was a lyric poet rather than a realistic one. Commenting on both articles in a review in the *Mainichi Shimbun* entitled "Shiki no Saikentō" [A Reevaluation of Shiki] on October 31, 1978, Ogata Tsutomu remarked that the history of haiku should be reexamined.

Chapter One

1. Yanagihara Kyokudō, *Yūjin Shiki* (Tokyo, 1946), pp. 31-32. Katō Tsunetada (pen-name Takusen) was born into the Ōhara family but later adopted by his maternal grandparents as their heir. After being in the foreign service for twenty years, he became a member of the Diet and of the Upper House (*Chokusen Kizokuin*), and mayor of Matsuyama City. He, Kanzan, and Shiki himself were the three most illustrious members of Shiki's family.

2. The *Chuang Tzu,* a Chinese work, is one of the classic texts of Taoism. It is said to have been written by a philosopher called Chuang Chou (tentatively 369–289 B.C.). See Burton Watson, tr., *Chuang Tzu: Basic Writings* (New York: Columbia University Press, 1969).

3. Herbert Spencer (1820–1903), the English philosopher and sociologist, most famous for *A System of Synthetic Philosophy.* His theories entered Japan in 1877 with Ozaki Yukio's translation *Kenri Teikō* and in 1882 with Noritake Kōtarō's translation *Shakaigaku no Genri.*

4. In 1890, Shiki asked Katō Tsunetada, then in Germany, to send him a book about aesthetics. Katō sent him Volume II of Eduard von Hartmann's

Aesthetik (Leipzig, 1887). Shiki, according to his own account, took the work to a friend who knew German, but even with the aid of the friend's word-by-word translation, found it made no sense to him at all. When a translation of the same work was later published in Mori Ōgai's magazine *Shigarami Zōshi,* Shiki bought the issue with great anticipation but again found that, because of the literalness of the translation, he could not make out the meaning.

5. I do not mean to imply that the conception of art as a unity and of poetry as something transcending genres had never existed before in Japan. The conception appears at least as far back as Bashō's famous statement in *Oi no Kobumi* [The Records of a Travel-Worn Satchel]: "One thread unites the waka of Saigyō, the linked verse of Sōgi, the paintings of Sesshū, the tea ceremony of Rikyū; for all art *(fūga)* follows the order of nature and makes the four seasons its friend." (Suguiura Shōichirō, Miyamoto Saburō, Ogino Kiyoshi, ed., *Bashō Bunshū.* Nihon Koten Bungaku Taikei 46 [Tokyo: Iwanami Shoten, 1968]).

Konishi Jinichi in *Nihon Bungakushi* (Tokyo, 1956), pp. 155-160, discusses the effect the introduction of Western ideas of literature had on the conception of literature in the Meiji period from a slightly different point of view.

6. The poem by Matsuo Bashō (1644-1694) is:

> furuike ya   The old pond!
> kawazu tobikomu   A frog jumps in—
> mizu no oto   the sound of water.

The poem by Kakinomoto Hitomaro (fl. ca. 680-700) is:

> ashihiki no   Shall I sleep alone
> yamadori no o no   on this endless night,
> shidari o no   long as the pheasant's tail
> naganagashi yo o   trailing through the hills?
> hitori ka mo nemu

(Although this poem appears in the eighth-century *Manyōshū,* the earliest extant collection of poetry in Japanese, no author is given. In the *Hyakunin Isshu* (ca. 1360), it is attributed to Hitomaro. Shiki must have read it there, rather than in the *Manyōshū.*)

7. Shiki did not record his reactions to reading *Ukigumo* [The Drifting

Cloud, 1887–1889] by Shōyō's disciple Futabatei Shimei. This novel is now considered Japan's first modern novel (see Marleigh Grayer Ryan, *Japan's First Modern Novel: Ukigumo of Futabatei Shimei* [New York: Columbia University Press, 1967]) and as such one might expect that it influenced Shiki. The only mention of it in his writings, however, seems to be in the series of articles he wrote for *Nippon* in 1893, *Bunkai Yatsu Atari* [Indiscriminate Attacks on the Literary World], where he discusses it in the context of the history of the Meiji novel. There he states that the Meiji novel began with *Portraits of Contemporary Students,* which was followed by three or four years of pallid imitations and then the appearance of *The Drifting Cloud,* about which he comments laconically: "*The Drifting Cloud,* being completely in the colloquial language [*genbunitchi*] achieved great precision of observation, illustrating what realism was."

One wonders when Shiki read the novel and what his more detailed reactions to it were. But in *The Snail House Near Tennōji* (the title is the name of Kōda Rohan's house), the uncompleted essay which set out to narrate Shiki's own reactions to the novels of his time as they appeared, he did not mention *The Drifting Cloud.* He emphasized, on the contrary, that the great excitement Shōyō's works roused in him did not make him seek out other contemporary novels. Instead, he retained a distance from the novel; he was not sure, he wrote, whether this was due to contempt or jealousy. Rohan's *The Romantic Buddha* was the next novel after *Portraits of Contemporary Students* to win his admiration. Although it was much talked about when it came out in 1889, he did not read it until the following year, when he came upon it by accident in a secondhand bookstore. Thus it seems quite possible that Shiki did not bother to read *The Drifting Cloud* when it was first published and that even when he did read it later, it corroborated his bent for realism rather than inspiring him with any fresh ideal.

8. The title *Talks on Haiku from the Otter's Den* was taken from *Dassai Shooku Shujin* [Master of the Otter's Den], one of Shiki's early pen names. By this name, Shiki alluded humorously to his habit of keeping a disorderly room filled with books and papers. The expression *dassaigyo* ("the otter enshrines fish"), originating in Chinese literature, was used to describe a writer who composed with many reference books spread out about him or who quoted a great deal from older works. Shiki, in humorous defense of his own sloppy habits, had once likened himself to the otter, saying, "I enshrine books and old scraps of paper—I'm not careless or capricious." From this his pen name had been born.

9. Until recently it was doubted that Shiki and Ōgai knew each other well, and not certain that they had even met. But Miyatsuchi Shin'ichi's

article "Shiki to Ōgai no Deai" [Shiki and Ōgai's Meeting] proved conclusively that they did meet in Shantung and engaged in lively literary discussions which left Ōgai with great admiration for Shiki.

10. While *A Drop of Ink* and *A Sixfoot Sickbed* were both written with the intention of publication and were serialized in *Nippon* as Shiki wrote them, *Stray Notes While Lying On My Back* was a strictly personal diary, only published posthumously.

11. Statues of the Guardian Deva Kings stand at the entrances to some Buddhist temples. They are very fierce-looking, with fat, muscular legs, and somewhat like Hercules in their associations with strength.

12. Kawahigashi Hekigotō, *Shiki Genkōroku* (Tokyo, 1936), pp. 715–22.

Chapter Two

1. Quoted in Kenneth B. Pyle, *The New Generation in Meiji Japan* (Stanford: Stanford University Press, 1969), p. 190.

2. In a letter to his disciple Kawahigashi Hekigotō of March 10, 1892, Shiki explained why he continued to write haiku although he thought the form doomed:

I hold the theory that we shall see the last of the haiku in the Meiji period. . . . However, I say this as a theorist. As an artist (and I include in this category all poets) it is better, on the contrary, to be ignorant of such ideas. Please don't pay attention to theories! (XVIII, 280)

3. In fact, even today the haiku's status as a serious art is periodically challenged, in spite of Shiki's efforts. The most famous modern attack on it was made by the scholar of French literature, Kuwabara Takeo (b. 1904) in his essay *Daini Geijutsu Ron: Gendai Haiku ni tsuite* [The Secondary Art of Modern Haiku: *Sekai*, November 1946. In Kuwabara Takeo (Kano Tsutomu and Patricia Murray, translators). *Japan and Western Civilization: Essays on Comparative Literature.* University of Tokyo Press, 1983.]

4. Translation of "natsugusa ya" poem by Donald Keene, in Donald Keene, ed., *Anthology of Japanese Literature* (Rutland, Vt., and Tokyo: Charles E. Tuttle Co., 1975), p. 369.

5. The *Kokinshū* [Collection of Ancient and Modern Times, ca. 905] was the first imperial anthology of Japanese court poetry.

Minamoto Sanetomo (1192–1219), assassinated at twenty-seven, was a Shōgun and student (in tanka) of Fujiwara Teika. He was associated with the revival of the *Manyōshū* style in the mid-classical period, and was greatly admired by two later *Manyōshū* enthusiasts, the scholar of National Studies Kamo no Mabuchi (1697–1769) and the modern tanka poet Saitō Mokichi (1882–1953). For a critical but worthwhile treatment of his importance in the history of Japanese poetry, see Robert H. Brower and Earl Miner, *Japanese Court Poetry* (Stanford, 1961), pp. 329–37.

6. This is a ludicrous attack, especially if one considers Shiki's own later poems; it can only be understood within the context of Shiki's temporary exaltation of imagination over realism in *The Haiku Poet Buson*.

7. The poet Hagiwara Sakutarō (1886–1942) in *Kyōshū no Shijin Yosa Buson* [Yosa Buson, Poet of Nostalgia. Shinchō Bunko, Shinchōsha, 1961. First published in 1936] and, more recently, the poet Andō Tsuguo (b. 1919) in *Yosa Buson* (Nihon Shijin Sen 18, Chikuma Shobō, 1970) have challenged Shiki's view of Buson as a poet of "positive beauty," showing that many of his poems deal with nostalgia and other themes associated, in Shiki's terms, with "negative beauty."

8. These are:

Naitō Meisetsu, Masaoka Shiki, Matsuse Seisei, Kawahigashi Hekigotō, Takahama Kyoshi, *Buson Kushū Kōgi*, 4 vols. (Haishodō, 1907).

Naitō Meisetsu et al., *Buson Ikō Kōgi* (Haishodō, 1905–1907).

Satō Kōroku, *Buson Haiku Hyōshaku* (Daigakkan, 1904).

9. After Shiki's death, his school split into two, one part led by Kyoshi and the other by Hekigotō. Leading poets emerged from both lines.

10. Shiki's belief that Bashō composed most of the poems of his last ten years about actual scenes is erroneous. From the diary of Bashō's companion Sora (which had not yet been discovered in Shiki's time) we know that much of *Oku no Hosomichi* is fictional. For example, Sora wrote that on the night he and Bashō were at Cape Izumo it was so stormy nothing could be seen. The most commonly accepted interpretation of the poem today is that it is not an objective description of a sight but that Bashō had in mind the many people exiled to Sado Island in times past and was identifying himself, a traveler far from home, with them.

11. *Shasei* was originally used by artists to translate the English "sketch" and French "dessin." After passing over into literature through Shiki, it was elaborated after his death, particularly by Takahama Kyoshi in the haiku and later by Saitō Mokichi in the tanka.

12. Kitazumi Toshio, *Shaseisetsu no Kenkyū* (Tokyo, 1968), pp. 27–28.

13. "Mature style," if someone whose life ended at the age of thirty-five can be said to have had one. But the fact that Shiki faced death early and with advance warning means that a certain process of maturation may have been, in fact seems to have been, telescoped in him.

14. Ōno Rinka, *Kindai Haiku no Kanshō to Hihyō* (Tokyo, 1967), pp. 23–24.

15. Donald Keene, in his invaluable *Japanese Literature: An Introduction for Western Readers* (New York: Grove Press, 1955), pp. 94–96, writes about the problem of individuality. Unfortunately, there is only room for a few excerpts from his discussion here, but the interested reader is referred to the whole:

Western literature in the late nineteenth century was dominated by the expression of individual impressions and beliefs. . . . In Japan there existed no such tradition of individualism, at least not since the civil wars of the twelfth century and afterwards had led to the formation of a rigid feudal society, where the claims of the individual were sternly denied. . . . In poetry too the prevailing note is one of impersonality, rather than that of the romantic cry from the poet's heart. . . . In the long centuries between Lady Murasaki's day and that of the late nineteenth century, there is seldom a voice that speaks to us with a truly personal note. . . . [T]he expression or creation of individuality remained, and I think still remains, the great problem.

16. Compare this poem to Bashō's:

hana no kumo	clouds of blossoms,
kane wa Ueno ka	a temple bell—
Asakusa ka	is it Ueno's? Asakusa's?

Here, too, spring haze is evoked by its effect upon the sound of a bell. It is hard not to believe that Shiki was influenced by this poem of Bashō's when he wrote his own, especially since Ueno is also mentioned in both poems.

Chapter Three

1. The *Kojiki* [Records of Ancient Matters, 712], with the *Nihon Shoki* [Chronicles of Japan, 720], is one of the early chronicles of Japan, containing most of the extant primitive verse.

2. *Hachidaishū* [Collection of Eight Eras] is the name for the first eight imperial anthologies of Japanese poetry, from the *Kokinshū*, ca. 905, through the *Shinkokinshū*, 1206.

3. Yanagihara Kyokudō, *Yūjin Shiki*, p. 118. This poem and the next are in neither the Kōdansha nor the Arusu *Shiki Zenshū*.

4. Ki no Tsurayuki (ca. 872–945), a leading tanka poet of the early

Heian period, one of the compilers of the *Kokinshū* and author of its Japanese preface as well as of the poem-diary *Tosa Nikki*.

5. Tayasu Munetake (1715–1771) was a tanka poet and scholar of National Learning during the mid-Tokugawa period, associated with Kamo no Mabuchi and the revival of the *Manyōshū*. He was one of the four poets whom Shiki felt particularly exemplified the principle of direct, realistic expression that was, to him, the essence of the *Manyōshū* style. The others were Sanetomo, Tachibana Akemi (1812–1868), and Hiraga Motoyoshi (1800–1865).

6. Saitō Mokichi and Tsuchiya Bunmei, eds., *Shiki Tanka Gappyō* (Tokyo, 1948), p. 17.

7. A more literal translation of the first three lines, making the redundancy clearer, would be: "brief sleep more and more painful, and painful the dream."

A pivot word (*kakekotoba*) is a word that modifies both what comes before and what comes after it. Although Shiki attacked the use of pivot words and other traditional forms of word-play in poetry, he used them himself on occasion, as Robert Brower has pointed out in "Masaoka Shiki and Tanka Reform", in Donald Shively, ed., *Tradition and Modernization in Japanese Culture* (Princeton, 1971).

8. Shiki was one of the early enthusiasts of baseball in Japan, and translated several of its terms into Japanese. He also took one of his early pen names from *yakyū* ("baseball,") reading it as *Noboru,* close to his given name of Noboru.

9. This is not to say that he always avoided such contrasts. For example the haiku *yomei/ikubaku ka aru/yo mijikashi* ("how much life/is left to me?/the night was short") derives its effect largely from the contrast between the Sino-Japanese of the first two lines and the pure Yamato words of the last line.

10. *Tabi* are a kind of sock worn with Japanese dress. They are usually tan, black, or white and made from cotton.

11. Yamaguchi Seishi in his brief essay on Shiki's haiku "Tennen to Ningen" is one exception.

12. The Kōdansha *Shiki Zenshū* gives the last line as *uta kangaetsutsu* ("while thinking of poetry") with *hitori fushi ori* ("I lie alone") as a variant. This is the form in which the poem appeared in *Stray Notes* (XI, 503). In the poem's earliest appearance, however, in *Nippon*, March 26, 1902, the last line was given as *hitori fushi ori* only; and this was also the text used by Saitō Mokichi in his discussion of the poem in *Masaoka Shiki*. Furthermore, the Arusu *Shiki Zenshū* (Arusu VI, 263) gives the last line as *hitori fushi ori* with *uta kangaetsutsu* as the variant. It is obviously impossible to say one text

is more accurate than the other when Shiki himself seems to have been unable
to make up his own mind, so I have used the text which seems to me to work
best as poetry.

13. *Shiki Zenshū,* Kōdansha, VI, 773.

14. Lady Sao (*Saogami*) is a female deity associated with spring.
According to Shiki's follower Saitō Mokichi (Mokichi et al., *Shiki Tanka
Gappyō,* p. 294), she is usually called *Saohime* (Princess Sao) and Shiki
probably coined the name *Saogami*. Mokichi, himself the major tanka poet
of the twentieth century, believed that this was the best tanka Shiki ever
wrote.

15. Harold Isaacson in *Peonies Kana* (New York, 1972), p. xiv, points
out that this haiku "burlesques statements found in Buddhist biographies that
while lotuses were in flower some person dying obtained birth in the Amida
Paradise, Sukhavati."

Chapter Four

1. By 1898, *Hototogisu* was the leading haiku magazine in Japan. Its
success may be gauged from the fact that the first Tokyo edition sold out the
day it was published and a second edition of 500 copies had to be printed.

2. At the traditional *tori no ichi* festival held each November at the Ō-
tori Shrine in Tokyo and at other temples and shrines as well, rakes said to
sweep in good luck and prosperity are sold in various sizes and prices.

3. Unless otherwise indicated, information about the *Yama kai* and the
history of the *shaseibun* movement in this paragraph is from Fukuda Kiyoto,
Shaseibunha no Kenkyū (Tokyo, 1972).

4. Tokuda Shūsei (1871–1943), one of those who suggested this, wrote
that it was the sketch from life writers such as Sōseki, Miekichi, Sachio, and
Kyoshi who had paved the way for the language of the modern novel, rather
than the naturalists (ibid, p. 6).

5. Shiga Naoya's statement quoted in Fukuda, p. 299. Shiba Ryōtarō's
opinion expressed in *Shiki Zenshū* XIII (Kōdansha, 1976), "Bunshō
Nihongo no Seiritsu to Shiki," p. 787.

6. There is no difference between descriptive prose (*jojibun*) and sketch
from life prose (*shaseibun*). Shiki also used the term *shajibun* ("realistic
prose"). All three terms are synonymous. I have used the term "sketch from
life prose" as consistently as possible in order to avoid confusion and because
it is the commonly used term today. Shiki himself, however, used the term
only once.

7. This is a complete translation but I have omitted the diagram of the

garden that accompanies the essay. In it, Shiki indicates each flower and plant by a haiku.

8. "My garden overgrown" is a line from the prose-poem *Kuei Ch'ü Lai Tz'u* by the Chinese poet T'ao Ch'ien (365–427).

9. Shiki was fond of the *Chuang Tzu* as a student and this passage may have been partly inspired by Chuang Chou's dream of the butterfly in that work:

Once Chuang Chou dreamt he was a butterfly, a butterfly flitting and fluttering around, happy with himself and doing as he pleased. He didn't know he was Chuang Chou. Suddenly he woke up and there he was, solid and unmistakeable Chuang Chou. But he didn't know if he was Chuang Chou who had dreamt he was a butterfly, or a butterfly dreaming he was Chuang Chou. Between Chuang Chou and a butterfly there must be *some* distinction! This is called the Transformation of Things. (*Chuang Tzu, Basic Writings,* tr. Burton Watson, p. 45).

10. "Lotus grass flowers" is my translation for *gengen no hana,* which is usually translated as "Chinese milk vetch." "Silver grass" is my translation for *susuki,* usually translated as "pampas grass."

11. This is Mori Ōgai, whom Shiki had met while in Shantung with the Japanese army in 1895.

Chapter Five

1. The *uta nikki* is a literary diary which uses poetry as well as prose to carry the narrative along. It has existed from A.D. 935 to the present. For detailed treatment of the genre and translated examples of the form, see Earl Miner, *Japanese Poetic Diaries.*

2. This idea is expressed openly in two tanka from another sequence in *A Drop of Ink:* the one about Lady Sao and that about building a trellis for moonflowers (see pp. 101-102).

3. The same impulse can be felt in such statements as this of 1898: "Even if I die, *Hototogisu* need not, of course; but the day *Hototogisu* dies will be the day of my own death. *Hototogisu* is my life."

4. Nakae Chōmin (1847–1901) was a scholar of French, a politician, and a critic. In 1901, told he had cancer of the larynx and only a year and a half to live, he put together a collection of short essays on a wide variety of subjects called *Ichinen Yūhan* [A Year and a Half]. After writing a sequel, *Zoku Ichinen Yūhan* [A Year and a Half Continued], which was also very

well received, he died at the end of 1901, having lived only several months since diagnosis of the disease. Shiki never met him in person, and knew him only through his books.

5. In May 1897, the pain in Shiki's pelvic region had become intense, and he became gravely ill.

6. The Cart of Fire was, according to Buddhist thought, the conveyance in which people traveled to the underworld.

7. Jizō is a Boddhissatva who lives in this world between Shakamuni's death and Miroku's advent, in order to influence human beings for the good. In popular belief, he is the guardian of those who die in childhood.

8. Onoe Kikugorō V (1844–1901) and Ichikawa Sadanji I (1842–1904) were, with Ishikawa Danjurō IX, the three most popular Kabuki actors of the Meiji period; the three were known for short as Dan-Kiku-Sa.

9. *Aki no hae* ("autumn fly") is a season word in haiku. By autumn the real fly season is over; those flies that are left move sluggishly and the equipment that goes with the summer fly season, such as fly-swatters, is broken. There is a sort of truce between flies and people. The poem well expresses this mood of calmness and subtly echoes Shiki's last remark in the passage immediately preceding.

10. The last line is probably addressed by the poet to himself. "To become a Buddha" means to die.

11. One possible interpretation of this poem is that as Shiki is dying, his face is pale as a moonflower and he is flatulent. It is based on the puns between *gao/kao* and *he/he* in yūgao no *kao/he*chima no *he. Yūgao* means "moonflower," *kao* means "face," *hechima* means "gourd," *he* means "fart."

12. "Autumn brocade" is a conventional tanka epithet for brightly colored autumn leaves. Shiki could not go outdoors to see the autumn leaves; the wallet was a substitute for them. Its contents (money) offered promise of at least gustatory delight, in place of the deeper joy that might be his could he walk among the many-colored scenes of autumn. The poem's tone, like many of Shiki's haiku on his illness, is ironic. It is reminiscent of the haiku that ends the March 20 entry of *A Drop of Ink:*

> byōshō ni   eating rice cakes everyday
> higoto mochi kuu   while sick in bed—
> Higan kana   that's my Higan! (XI, 143)

Higan refers both to the Buddhist ceremony which takes place at the vernal and autumnal equinoxes, and also "the shores of paradise." The vernal equinox took place on March 20, and it was the custom to eat rice cakes to celebrate it, so this is the primary meaning of the term here; but since Shiki was a glutton about food, he is also using the term in the second sense, humorously, indicating his delight at having an excuse to gorge on rice cakes. At the same time, there is a note of sadness and self-pity to the poem, since he has to celebrate the holiday in bed.

Selected Bibliography

PRIMARY SOURCES

1. Collected Works of Masaoka Shiki in Japanese. Place of publication for all works listed is Tokyo. There are three editions of Shiki's collected works:

Samukawa, Sokotsu, et al., eds. *Shiki Zenshū.* 15 volumes, Arusu, 1924–1926. A beautifully produced edition but not as complete as the next.

Kawahigashi, Hekigotō, et al., eds. *Shiki Zenshū.* 22 volumes, Kaizōsha, 1929–1931. More complete than the Arusu edition, but not as complete as the next.

Masaoka, Chūsaburō, et al., eds. *Shiki Zenshū.* 22 volumes of Shiki's work and three supplementary volumes of secondary works. Kōdansha, 1975–1978. The best of all the collected works so far. Painstakingly assembled to include much new material not known before, its texts based on comparisons to all known versions, and including much supplementary material as well as copious illustrations.

There are also several one-volume collections of Shiki's selected works. I have found the most useful to be, in order of publication:

Samukawa, Sokotsu, ed. *Masaoka Shiki Shū.* Gendai Nihon Bungaku Zenshū 11. Kaizōsha, 1928. The most comprehensive of the editions of selected works.

Keene, Donald, et al., eds. *Ishikawa Takuboku. Masaoka Shiki. Takahama Kyoshi.* Nihon no Bungaku 15. Chūō Kōronsha, 1967. A good selection of Shiki's poetry, criticism, and diaries, with some notes, and a valuable essay (*Kaisetsu*) on all three authors. Also has Kyoshi's biographical novel about Shiki, *Kaki Futatsu.*

Matsui, Toshihiko, ed. *Masaoka Shiki Shū.* Nihon Kindai Bungaku Taikei 16. Kadokawa Shoten, 1972. Tanka, haiku, and prose. More of the critical writings and less of the diaries than Keene's edition. Has extensive notes and lengthy bibliography.

Illustrations for all the collected works, but especially the Arusu edition, include examples of Shiki's calligraphy, sketches, and paintings. Fuller selections, however, are available in several specialized works. One of the best is:

Yamakami, Jirō, compiler. *Shiki Iboku.* 3 volumes. Kyūryūdō, 1975. A lavishly produced selection of Shiki's calligraphy, paintings and sketches, with accompanying essays by Ōoka Makoto, Yamamoto Kenkichi, and the compiler.

2. A Finding List

Following is a list of Shiki's works referred to in this book, arranged alphabetically by translated title, with the numbers of the volumes in which they may be found in the Arusu *Shiki Zenshū* (abbreviated "A") and the Kōdansha *Shiki Zenshū* (abbreviated "K").

A Dream (Yume). A, X; K, XII.

A Drop of Ink (Bokujū Itteki). A, VII; K, XI.

After Death (Shigo). A, X; K, XII.

A Sixfoot Sickbed (Byōshō Rokushaku). A, VII; K, XI.

A Summer Ten Years Ago (Jūnen Mae no Natsu). A, XIV; K, XII.

Basho's Surprise (Bashō no Ikkyō). A, IV; K, IV.

The Capital by Moonlight (Tsuki no Miyako). A, X; K, XIII.

Citron Miso Society (Yumiso Kai). A, X; K, XII.

Classified Collection of Haiku (Haiku Bunrui). 12 volumes. Arusu, 1928–1929 (not included in any *Shiki Zenshū*).

The Cloak of Invisibility (Kakuremino). A, VIII; K, XIII.

Cloud Diary (Kumo no Nikki). A, X; K, XII.

Cold Mountain, Fallen Trees (Kanzan Rakuboku). A, I, II, III; K, I, II, III, XXI.

Descriptive Prose (Jojibun). A, V; K, XIV.

The Elements of Haiku (Haikai Taiyō). A, IV; K, IV.

First Dream (Hatsuyume). A, X; K, XII.

For the Beginning of Hototogisu, Volume IV, Number 1 (Hototogisu Daiyonkan Daiichigo no Hajime ni). A, XIV; K, V.

Fruit (Kudamono). A, X; K, XII.

Haiku Manuscripts (Haiku Kō). A, III; K, III.

The Haiku Poet Buson (Haijin Buson). A, IV; K, IV.

Haiku Wastebasket (Haikai Hogukago). A, IV; K, IV.

The Haiku World of 1896 (Meiji Nijūkunen no Haiku Kai). A, IV; K, IV.

Indiscriminate Attacks on the Literary World (Bunkai Yatsu Atari). A, V; K, XIV.

The Lamp's Shadow (Rampu no Kage). A, X; K, XII.
Letters. A, IX (1888–1897), XV (1898-1902; date unknown); K, XVIII
    (1888–1895), XIX (1896–1902; date unknown).
Letters to a Tanka Poet (Utayomi ni Atauru Sho). A, V; K, VII.
Literature (Bungaku). A, V; K, XIV.
Love (Koi). A, XIV; K, XII.
The Morning of September 14 (Kugatsu Jūyokka no Asa). A, X; K, XII.
My Sickness (Waga Yamai). A, X: K, XIII.
On Western Dogs (Yōken Setsu). Not in A; K, IX.
The Origin and Development of Poetry (Shiika no Kigen oyobi Hensen). A,
    VIII; K, IX.
Painting (E). A, XIV; K, XII.
Poems from the Bamboo Village (Take no Sato Uta). A, VI; K, VI.
Rakes and Lanterns (Kumade to Chōchin). A, X; K, XII.
Random Questions and Random Answers (Zuimon Zuitō). A, XIII; K, V.
Record of the Hanging Bridge (Kakehashi no Ki). A, X; K, XIII.
Record of the Little Garden (Shōen no Ki). A, X; K, XII.
*Reflections Occasioned by the Publication of Volume One of Selections from
    the Haiku Notebooks of the Otter's Den (Dassai Shooku Haiwa
    Chōshō Jōkan o Shuppan Suru ni Tsukite Omoitsukitaru Tokoro o
    Iu)*. Not in A; K, V.
Sake (Sake). A, X; K, XII.
Scattered Remarks on Literature (Bungaku Mangen). A, V; K, XIV.
Scribblings (Fude Makase). A, VIII; K, IX.
Sickness (Yamai). A, X; K, XII.
Sights from a Rickshaw (Shajō Shoken). A, X; K, XII.
The Snail House Near Tennōji (Tennōji Han no Kagyūro). A, XIV; K,
    XII.
Some Remarks on Bashō (Bashō Zōdan). A, IV; K, IV.
Sounds of a Summer Night (Natsu no Yo no Oto). A, X; K, XII.
Spring Scenes from a Rickshaw (Shajō no Shunkō). A, X; K, XII.
Stray Notes While Lying On My Back (Gyōga Manroku). A, VII; K, XI.
Strong Japanese Prose (Tsuyoki Wabun). A, V; K, XIV.
Talks on Haiku from the Otter's Den (Dassai Shooku Haiwa). A, IV; K,
    IV.
Ten Poems in a Hundred (Hyakuchū Jisshu). Nippon, February 27–March
    8, 1898; March 10, 12, 1898. Kōdansha *Shiki Zenshū* VI, 115–208,
    has revised versions of these poems as they appeared in *Poems from the
    Bamboo Village* with notes indicating what the original versions were.
Travel (Tabi). A, X; K, XII.

The Voyager-Poet Bashō (Angya Haijin Bashō). A, XIII; K, IV.
Waiting for Lunch (Meshi Matsu Aida). A, X; K, XII.
Words of Pain from a Sickbed (Byōshō Kugo). A, XIV; K, XII.

3. Collections of Shiki's Poetry

The collections of Shiki's haiku are:

Kanzan Rakuboku [Cold Mountain, Fallen Trees], in which Shiki collected
the 12,700 haiku he wrote between 1885 and 1896.

Haiku Kō [Haiku Manuscripts], in which he collected the 5,356 haiku he
wrote from 1897 through 1900 as well as some from 1901.

Dassai Shooku Haiku Chōshō Jōkan [Selections from the Haiku Notebooks of
the Otter's Den, Volume One], which consisted of selections made
by Shiki from his haiku of 1892–1896 in *Cold Mountain, Fallen
Trees.*

Of the three collections above, only the last was published in Shiki's lifetime,
in April 1902, by Haishodō. The other two were first published in the
Arusu, *Shiki Zenshū* (1924–1926), and later in subsequent editions of
Shiki's works. The haiku of 1902 were only collected and published
posthumously, again first as part of his complete works.

In contrast to the three collections of Shiki's haiku, which include about
18,000 poems, there is only one of his tanka, *Take no Sato Uta* [Poems
from the Bamboo Village; "Man from the Bamboo Village" was the
pen-name Shiki used for tanka], and it includes only about 2,000
poems. This collection also was only published posthumously, in 1904,
by Haishodō, as Volume 5 of *Shiki Ikō* [Shiki's Posthumous Manu-
scripts]. Edited by Itō Sachio on the basis of Shiki's own manuscript of
the same title, it included poems from 1897 through 1902. After
Sachio's death, Shiki's original manuscript was lost until 1954. In 1956,
a new edition, which reproduced Shiki's original manuscript and was
thus more complete than Sachio's edition, was published by Iwanami
Shoten, edited by Tsuchiya Bunmei and Gomi Yasuyoshi. Sachio's
edition had 544 tanka, fifteen *chōka,* and twelve *sedōka,* whereas
Shiki's own manuscript had 1,933 waka and also *shintaishi* and *hauta.*
The Kōdansha *Shiki Zenshū* includes not only Shiki's original manuscript but the poems he omitted from it as well.

SECONDARY SOURCES

The most complete and up-to-date bibliography of works about Shiki is in
Matsui Toshihiko, *Masaoka Shiki no Kenkyū* (2 volumes, Meiji

Shoin, 1976), Vol. 2, pp. 644–727. This work is also the closest there
is to a definitive treatment of Shiki's life and works. The great number
of works about Shiki is evident from the length of Matsui's bibliography,
and there would be no point in trying to duplicate his completeness
here. Instead, I have listed works of three kinds: those exclusively about
Shiki; those not exclusively about Shiki but which contain valuable
information about him and his work and place him in perspective, such
as general works on the history of the tanka or the haiku; and a few
lesser-known works which, while not basic, I found especially valuable
for their insights. All works were published in Tokyo.

It should be mentioned that there is a Shiki Studies Society (*Ehime Daigaku
Shiki Kenkyū Kai*) at Ehime University in Matsuyama, Shiki's birth-
place. Since 1970, it has published intermittently a periodical devoted to
Shiki studies, *Masaoka Shiki Shiryō to Kenkyū*. As of November 1978,
five issues had appeared. Shiki is also one of the protagonists of Shiba
Ryōtarō's four-volume best-selling historical novel *Saka no Ue no Kumo*
[Clouds on the Hilltop, Bungei Shunjū, 1970–1971], and the same
author's *Hitobito no Ashioto* [The Sound of Peoples' Footsteps, Chūō
Kōron, 1981].

1. Works About Shiki by His Disciples and Followers

Kawahigashi, Hekigotō, compiler. *Shiki Genkōroku*. Seikyōsha, 1936.
Reminiscences of Shiki by his family and friends. Gives a sense of
intimacy with Shiki himself and the period he lived in.

Naitō, Meisetsu and **Takahama, Kyoshi.** *Shiki Kushū Kōgi*. Haishodō,
1916. Explications of Shiki's haiku, by two of his leading disciples.

Saitō, Mokichi. *Masaoka Shiki*. Sōgensha, 1946. (Reprinted in *Saitō
Mokichi Zenshū*, V. 20, Iwanami Shoten, 1973.) Illuminating and
original critical biography of Shiki as poet, critic, and diarist by the
leading tanka poet of the twentieth century.

———, and **Tsuchiya Bunmei,** eds. *Shiki Tanka Gappyō*. Araragi Sōsho
114, Seijisha, 1948. Shiki's followers in informal discussions of
individual tanka. Poets on poetry, and illuminating in ways that no
scholar can match.

Samukawa, Sokotsu. "Shiki Koji no Haiku Kenkyū." *Haiku Kōza 5:
Kanshō Hyōshaku Hen*. Edited by Yamamoto Mitsuo. Kaizōsha, 1932.
Some helpful remarks on various of Shiki's haiku.

Yamaguchi, Seishi. "Tennen to Ningen." Haiku Geppō No. 14: Masaoka
Shiki. Bound with Matsui Toshihiko, *Masaoka Shiki*. The earliest

article, to my knowledge, to point out that Shiki's later sketch from life haiku were not only descriptions of nature, but also described himself.

Yanagihara, Kyokudō, *Yūjin Shiki.* Maeda Shuppansha, 1946. A reminiscence of Shiki by a member of the Wind in the Pines Society and the first editor of *Hototogisu.*

2. By Contemporary Writers

Beichman, Janine. "Kaigai ni okeru Shiki kenkyū." In *Shiki Zenshū,* V, Geppō 13. Kōdansha, 1976. Summarizes Shiki studies outside Japan up to 1976.

———. "Masaoka Shiki no kōseki." *Eigo Bungaku Sekai* XI, 3 (June 1976). Asserts that Shiki's originality as a haiku critic lay in his insistence that haiku was a part of literature rather than in his stress on realism.

———. "Sanbunteki na shi to shiteki na sanbun." In *Shiki Zenshū,* IV, Geppō 8. Kōdansha, 1975. Contends that Shiki's most moving writing lies on the border between poetry and prose.

———. "Shiki no inochi to shizen." *Haiku* XXVI, 9 (September 1977). Japanese version of Chapter 3, section III, of this book.

Fujikawa, Chūji. *Masaoka Shiki.* Kindai Tanka Shiriizu: Hito to Sakuhin 7. Ōfūsha, 1963. Treats the life and works with emphasis on the tanka.

Fukuda, Kiyoto and Maeda Tomi. *Masaoka Shiki.* Shimizu Shoin, 1968. Biography, with coverage of the works as well.

Katsura, Taizō. "Shinkō Meiji Kadanshi no Koshō." In *Kaikoku Hyakunen Kinen: Meiji Bunkashi Ronshū.* Edited by Kaikoku Hyakunen Kinen Bunka Jigyōkai. Kangensha, 1952. A little-known article that explains how Shiki's friendships with conservative writers of tanka and Chinese poetry (*kanshi*) influenced his attitudes toward the *Manyōshū.*

Keene, Donald. "Kaisetsu." In *Ishikawa Takuboku. Masaoka Shiki. Takahama Kyoshi.* Edited by Donald Keene. Nihon no Bungaku 15. Chūō Kōronsha, 1967. Japanese version of "Shiki and Takuboku" (see English-language bibliography). Reprinted in the same author's *Nihon no Sakka,* Chūō Kōronsha, 1972.

———. "Masaoka Shiki." In *Nihon Bungaku no Sanpo.* Asahi Shimbunsha, 1975. Brief, but full of information and insights.

Kobori, Keiichirō. "Iken Hitotsu." *Dōgyū.* February 1972. Reports on Keene's interpretation of the first verse of the tanka sequence on the wisteria (see my Chapter 5), which has influenced my own interpretation of the sequence.

Kubota, Masafumi. *Masaoka Shiki*. Jimbutsu Sōsho 144. Yoshikawa Kō-
    bunkan, 1967. A good biography of Shiki.

Kusumoto, Kenkichi. *Masaoka Shiki*. Short essays on different aspects of
    Shiki as man and poet; includes material on the state of the haiku just
    prior to Shiki's reform.

Matsui, Toshihiko. *Masaoka Shiki*. Haiku Shiriizu: Hito to Sakuhin 4.
    Ōfūsha, 1969. Excellent biography of Shiki. Extensive notes and
    commentary for many of the haiku.

Miyatsuchi, Shin'Ichi. "Shiki to Ōgai no Deai." In *Shiki Zenshū*, XII,
    Geppō 7. Kōdansha, 1975. Offers the first conclusive proof that Shiki
    and Ōgai knew each other.

Ōoka, Makoto. *Shiki Kyoshi*. Kashinsha, 1976. Essays on Shiki and Kyoshi
    by a leading modern poet and critic. See the same author's remarks
    about Shiki in *Ki no Tsurayuki*. Nihon Shijin Sen 7. Chikuma Shobō,
    1971, pp. 5-33.

————. "Kakushinka Shiki to Kajin Shiki." In *Shiki Zenshū*, VI. Kō-
    dansha, 1977, pp. 753-73. Sensitive treatment of Shiki as a tanka poet.

Takagi, Kiyoko. "Masaoka Shiki no Sei to Shi." In *Nihonjin no Seishikan*.
    Edited by Shūkyō Shisō Kenkyūkai. Daizō Sensho 9. Daizō Shuppan,
    1972. Shiki from the viewpoint of a scholar of religion.

Yamamoto, Kenkichi. *Shiki to Kyoshi*. Kawade Shobō, 1976. Essays by a
    leading modern critic on Shiki and Kyoshi.

3. Other Works

Andō, Tsuguo. "*Hyakunin Isshu* Hyōshaku." *Taiyō: Bessatsu Hyakunin
    Isshu* 1 (Winter 1972). Heibonsha. Commentary on the *Hyakunin
    Isshu* by a modern poet; several of the poems were discussed by Shiki in
    his *Letters to a Tanka Poet*, and where their interpretations disagree,
    Andō discusses the differences, thus shedding light on both the poems
    themselves and Shiki's thinking.

Etō, Jun. *Sōseki to Sono Jidai*. 2 volumes. Shinchōsha, 1970. A biography
    of Sōseki, but contains much material on Shiki and on the friendship of
    the two writers.

Fukuda, Kiyoto. *Shaseibunha no Kenkyū*. Meiji Shoin, 1972. Excellent
    treatment of the development of the sketch from life style from Shiki to
    the contemporary period, in essays, short stories and novels.

Hisamatsu, Senichi. *Nihon Bungaku Hyōronshi: Kinsei Kindai Hen*.
    Shibundō, 1952. Discusses Shiki's criticism in the context of general
    history of literary theory and criticism in premodern and modern
    periods.

Katsumine, Shinpū. *Shiki Izen no Meiji Haikai*. Tōbundō, 1935. The
    haiku world of the early Meiji period just prior to Shiki.

Kimata, Osamu. *Kindai Tanka no Kanshō to Hihyō.* Meiji Shoin, 1954. Useful explications of famous modern tanka, including several of Shiki's.

Kitazumi, Toshio. *Shaseiha Kajin no Kenkyū.* Hōbunkan, 1959. Studies in Shiki as tanka poet and of his followers in tanka, with emphasis on the sketch from life.

———. *Shaseisetsu no Kenkyū.* Revised edition. Kadokawa Shoten, 1968. Studies in the sketch from life.

Koizumi, Tōzō. *Kindai Tankashi: Meiji Hen.* Hakuyōsha, 1955. History of the tanka in the Meiji period.

Konishi, Jinichi. *Haiku: Hassei Yori Gendai Made.* Kenkyūsha Gakusei Bunko. Kenkyūsha Shuppan, 1952. A general history of the haiku, with perceptive and original remarks on several haiku by Shiki. Revised edition: *Haiku no Sekai:Hassei yori Gendai made.* Kenkyūsha Shuppan, 1981.

———. *Nihon Bungakushi.* Kōbundō, 1956.

Kubota, Masafumi. *Kindai Tanka no Kōzō.* Nagata Shobō, 1970. Essays on the formation of the modern tanka.

Matsui, Toshihiko. *Kindai Haironshi.* Haiku Shiriizu: Hito to Sakuhin, Bekkan. Ōfūsha, 1969. Detailed history of modern haiku theory and criticism from the early Meiji period on.

Nakamura, Fusetsu. *Fusetsu Haiga.* Introduction by Natsume Sōseki, haiku by Kawahigashi Hekigotō, commentary by Takahama Kyoshi. 2nd printing. Kōkadō, 1910. Haiku drawings by the artist who influenced the development of Shiki's sketch from life.

Ōno, Rinka. *Kindai Haiku no Kanshō to Hihyō.* Meiji Shoin, 1967. Excellent explications for the most highly valued modern haiku, including several by Shiki.

Shinma, Shin'ichi. *Kindai Kadanshi.* Hanawa Shobō, 1968. Succinct history of the modern tanka.

Tanaka, Junji. *Kindai Tanka Kanshōshū.* Kindai Tanka Shiriizu: Hito to Sakuhin 10. Ōfūsha, 1965. Explications of famous modern tanka including several of Shiki's. The author summarizes the history of critical opinion about each tanka that he discusses.

4. In English

Shiki was first introduced to English-speaking readers in 1911, when a few translations of his haiku appeared in William Porter's *A Year of Japanese Epigrams,* one of the earliest collections of haiku in English translation. Since then, about fifty works, chiefly on the haiku, have mentioned him in passing, while a few have more substantial selections from his haiku. It is only in approximately the last fifteen years, however, that the English-speaking reader has had much chance to read either Shiki's tanka or his prose.

This section lists only those works that have a substantial amount of Shiki's writing in them, deal with him at length, or are useful for placing him in context. Readers who wish a more extensive listing that includes works referring only peripherally to Shiki may refer to J. Thomas Rimer and Robert E. Morrell, *Guide to Japanese Poetry*. Boston: G. K. Hall and Co., 1975.

Beichman-Yamamoto, Janine. "Masaoka Shiki's *A Drop of Ink.*" *Monumenta Nipponica* XXX, 3 (1975). Much of the introductory material is repeated in this book, but the translation of the diary itself is more complete.

Blyth, R. H. *Haiku.* 4 volumes. Tokyo: Hokuseido Press, 1949–1952.

————. *History of Haiku.* 2 volumes. Tokyo: Hokuseido Press, 1963–1964. Both works are comprehensive treatments of the nature and history of the haiku, with copious examples, including many of Shiki's haiku and extracts from his critical writings. The author has a very strong conviction that the essence of haiku is mystical, and this colors many of his interpretations, including his disapproval of Shiki.

Brower, Robert H., and Miner, Earl. *Japanese Court Poetry.* Stanford: Stanford University Press, 1961. Although Shiki is mentioned only twice (pp. 335 and 395), the work as a whole is indispensable for an understanding of the poetic tradition in the context of which Shiki's tanka reform took place.

Brower, Robert H. "Masaoka Shiki and Tanka Reform." In *Tradition and Modernization in Japanese Culture.* Edited by Donald H. Shively. Princeton: Princeton University Press, 1971. The first lengthy critical work in English devoted to an evaluation of Shiki's tanka reform and tanka poetry. Especially illuminating on his debt to classical court tanka.

Henderson, Harold. *An Introduction to Haiku.* Garden City, N.Y.: Doubleday, 1958. Treats Shiki as haiku poet and critic, and has translations of forty-three poems, eight of which are reprinted in Donald Keene, compiler and editor, *Modern Japanese Literature, an anthology.* Rutland, Vt.: Tuttle, 1965.

Isaacson, Harold J., translator and editor. *Peonies Kana: Haiku by the Upasaka Shiki.* New York: Theatre Arts Books, 1972. Translations of many of Shiki's haiku arranged by season and with explanatory notes. I question the retention of the Japanese *kireji* ("cutting words") in the English translations, the emphasis on the posthumous title *koji* (upasaka) and the inclusion of a Noh play only because it has the word *koji* in the title. Many of the explanatory notes are quite useful, however, and the selection of poems represents Shiki's range very fully.

Keene, Donald. "Shiki and Takuboku." In *Landscapes and Portraits: Appreciations of Japanese Culture.* Tokyo and Palo Alto: Kōdansha International Ltd.,˙1971. Rounded portrait of Shiki as tanka poet, haiku poet, diarist, and critic and comparison of him with Ishikawa Takuboku. Like Brower's essay, it differs in important points from accepted Japanese critical opinion, finding Shiki more traditional than commonly supposed.

Kimata, Osamu. "Shiki Masaoka: His Haiku and Tanka." *Philosophical Studies of Japan,* VIII, 1967. (Compiled by Japanese National Commission for UNESCO and published by Nippon Gakujutsu Shinkōkai.) A study of Shiki as a haiku and tanka poet.

Miner, Earl. "The Verse Record of My Peonies." In *Japanese Poetic Diaries.* Berkeley and Los Angeles: University of California Press, 1969. Excellent translation of and essay on *Botan Kuroku* [The Verse Record of My Peonies], a short poetic diary that Shiki wrote in 1899, in the context of a discussion of the poetic diary in Japanese literature and translations of earlier examples.

Nippon Gakujutsu Shinkōkai, Special Haiku Committee of Japanese Classics Translation Committee consisting of Asō Isoji et al. *Haikai and Haiku.* Tokyo: Nippon Gakujutsu Shinkōkai, 1958. Extensive selection of haiku including several by Shiki with material setting him in historical context.

Ueda, Makoto. *Modern Japanese Haiku: An Anthology.* Tokyo: University of Tokyo Press, 1976. Twenty haiku by Shiki, with brief biography and longer introduction. Covers many more modern haiku poets than any other anthology.

Yasuda, Kenneth. *The Japanese Haiku: Its Essential Nature, History, and Possibilities in English, with Selected Examples.* Rutland, Vt.: Tuttle, 1957. A useful introduction to the haiku with several excerpts from Shiki's haiku criticism and translations of his haiku.

Index

The first lines of poems and the titles of poem sequences are in quotes; unless otherwise indicated in parentheses after the line or title, all are by Shiki.

The titles of prose works and collections of poetry are in italics. Unless otherwise indicated in parentheses, all are by Shiki.